Your Small Business Made Simple

Richard R. Gallagher, D.B.A.

Edited and prepared for publication by The Stonesong Press, Inc.

A MADE SIMPLE BOOK

DOUBLEDAY

NEW YORK   LONDON   TORONTO   SYDNEY   AUCKLAND

Edited and prepared for publication by The Stonesong Press
Managing Editor: Sheree Bykofsky
Editor: Lillian R. Rodberg
Design: Blackbirch Graphics, Inc.

Published by Doubleday, a division of
Bantam Doubleday Dell Publishing Group, Inc.
666 Fifth Avenue, New York, New York 10103

MADE SIMPLE and DOUBLEDAY are trademarks of Doubleday,
a division of Bantam Doubleday Dell Publishing
Group, Inc.

Library of Congress Cataloging-in-Publication Data
Gallagher, Richard R.
  Your small business made simple.

  A MADE SIMPLE BOOK
  Includes index.
  1. New business enterprises.   2. Small business.
I. Title.
HD62.5.G35   1989   658'.022   88-33466
ISBN 0-385-23742-1

CONTENTS

PART ONE

GETTING OFF TO A GOOD START

CHAPTER ONE

Free Enterprise, the Profit Motive, and You

KEY TERMS

capitalism
entrepreneurship
free enterprise system
laissez-faire

locus of security
loss
marketing
profit

Henry Ford, tinkering in his garage with the horseless carriage that evolved into the fabled "Tin Lizzie" ... Lane Bryant, stitching maternity dresses for herself and her friends, on her way to becoming a retailing byword ... the entrepreneur who becomes a household word and makes millions in the process is an American tradition: maybe you're thinking of becoming the next Henry Ford or Lane Bryant.

Maybe you're thinking in much more modest terms, of combining an independent lifestyle with earning a living that equals or betters what you could earn working for others. Or maybe you're thinking of working for yourself part-time while rearing a family or enjoying your retirement. Whatever your small-business dream, you're in good company.

Entrepreneurship: On the Upsurge

"Going into business for myself" ha long been part of the American Drea' Our political and economic system is of free enterprise, or **capitalism.** In a italist system, individuals (alone groups), not the government, accumulate savings and invest them in the tools of production—factories, machinery, everything needed to produce products and services—in the hope of making a profit. **Profit** is what is left after all expenses of a business—including management compensation—have been deducted. Profit is your return on your investment and the reward for the risk you take in starting an enterprise, nurturing it through its difficult early years, and keeping it growing. Profit is your indicator that your business is succeeding. Just as wages reward a laborer's efforts, rent rewards landlords, and interest rewards lenders, profit is the business owner's personal reward for the money, time, effort, and creativity invested in the enterprise.

The other side of profit is **loss.** In its simplest sense, entrepreneurship consists of risking the loss of money, time, and effort in the hope—but without any guarantee—of profit.

In a **free enterprise system,** anyone who has the capital (from a few hundred dollars to a few million), the time, and the expertise to do so can embark on any business he or she chooses. Although there are many government regulations concerning business—local, county, state, and federal—no American is legally prevented from starting any legitimate enterprise. Provided that you do not use another's name, product design, or trademark, you are free to compete with any existing business, just as you are free to start something entirely new. Millions of Americans have made use of this freedom.

Moreover, **entrepreneurship**—owning one's own business—is on the rise. Despite all the publicity about multinational corporations and megabillion-dollar conglomerates, both the number and the proportion of U.S. businesses with fewer than 100 employees keep growing: to 14 million in a recent count. More people are employed by small businesses than by large. And between 1980 and 1988, when major U.S. corporations cut their payrolls by some 3.1 million workers, small companies created more than 17 million new full-time and part-time jobs.

From Home Business to Household Word

The stories are part of American folklore. Ford and his Tin Lizzie . . . Steve Jobs and his Apple Computer . . . Ray Kroc and McDonald's. Some are less well known. In the 1920s, dressmaker Ida Rosenthal gave away the first brassieres to clients who liked the way they made the clothes fit. Today's Maidenform Company grew out of her innovation. Two men and a few workers selling abrasive sand developed an adhesive for gluing the sand. Their Minnesota Mining and Manufacturing company became today's giant 3M. Margaret Rudkin, baking bread to make ends meet in the late 1940s, started Pepperidge Farm (now owned by the Campbell Company—a giant that evolved from another, earlier home kitchen).

And today? With the 1990s on the horizon, *Newsweek* estimates that 2 million U.S. men and women are millionaires. Of these, the newsmagazine reports, nearly 90 percent have earned their fortune by starting their own firms.

Not all small businesses succeed on this scale. Many fail—some in their first year of operation. Fewer than half survive their first five years. The publication *Business Week Careers* puts it this way: "If there is a first law of entrepreneurial thinking, it is undoubtedly this: Risks are directly proportional to rewards." It's natural to think about the potential rewards. But it's just as important to consider, and minimize, your risks.

Most business experts believe that the small enterprises that fail do so largely because their owners did not do enough planning. Most especially, they failed to allow themselves enough start-up funds to get them through the crucial first year. You've taken the first step in avoiding that kind of failure by buying this book. In the chapters to follow you'll learn the basic steps that will get your business off to a successful start.

One point to remember is that no matter how carefully you plan your business, how great you believe your product or service is, or how vigorously you try to sell it, in the end the consumer, not you, will determine how successful you are. Free enterprise applies to the customer as well as to the businessperson. The government can't close your business unless you break the law, but the public can close your business simply by staying away. Consumers are free to buy—or not to buy—whatever and from whomever they choose. Finding out what consumers want or need and then making them aware that you are providing for that need is called **marketing.** A well-thought-out marketing plan is crucial to your success, and several chapters in this book are devoted to your marketing program.

Legalities and Formalities

The U.S. system is basically free enterprise, but it is not **laissez-faire** ("leave it alone"). Restrictions, legalities, and regulations surround any business enterprise. Of course, it's completely illegal to manufacture or sell certain kinds of drugs, practice medicine or nursing without a license, sell stock in nonexistent companies, or ship contraband. Apart from that, many kinds of businesses require licenses. There are business taxes you must pay, rules of employment you must follow, and regulations about hours, sanitation, and use of the environment.

We'll be talking about licensing, taxes, and other government regulations in later chapters. Don't be frightened by those regulations or immobilized by not knowing how to meet them. Some businesses require no permits at all; the requirements for others are minimal. Use the tips in this book as your guideline.

But before you do, you should answer a question that's more important even than those related to your market. Is small business really for you?

Is Entrepreneurship For You?

Factors you need to consider are your background, your financial and personal resources, your knowledge of people and their needs and desires, and your general attitude toward business and life. Take a few minutes to respond to the questionnaire in the box. Then think over your answers in relation to the discussion below.

IS OWNING A SMALL BUSINESS FOR ME?

Answer each question "yes" or "no"; then tally your answers.

What About Me?

○ Can I get a new idea started and make it work?
○ Do I want my own business enough to work long hours without being sure how much, if anything, I'll be paid?
○ Have I worked for someone else in the kind of business I want to start?
○ Have I supervised other people successfully?
○ Have I had any training in business management?
○ Has anyone in my family been an entrepreneur?
○ Can I discipline myself to get work done?
○ Am I willing to take calculated risks, then work all-out for success?

What About My Customers?

○ Do I have a clear image of who will buy my product or service?
○ Is the population where I live large enough to support my product or service?
○ Do people need what I'm offering, or do I just think they might?
○ Are most businesses in my community doing well?
○ Are businesses like mine doing well elsewhere in the country?

It's unlikely that you answered all the questions with "yes." Which did you answer with "no"? Those "no" answers should direct your attention to areas where you need more information or help. You might want to highlight those areas for particular attention as you work your way through this book.

One important area over which you have no control is your own personality and background. Is there such a thing as an entrepreneurial personality? It seems so. Certain traits of character and background occur over and over again in successful entrepreneurs. *Business Week* found, for example, that most come from homes where at least one parent was self-employed. Most showed entrepreneurial instincts very early—by serving a paper route, sitting babies or pets, mowing lawns, or something similar. Nearly two thirds were the oldest child in their fam-

What About Money?

○ Do I know how much money I need to get started?

○ Have I calculated—in writing—how much of my own money I can put into this business?

○ Have I determined how much credit I can get from suppliers (the people I will buy from)?

○ Do I know where I can borrow the rest of my start-up money?

○ Have I figured out how much income I expect the business to earn for me?

○ Have two or three others in similar businesses told me this amount is reasonable?

○ Have I planned on a salary for myself in addition to any profit the business might make?

○ Will I be able to live and pay my bills if I can draw nothing from the business for six months? For a year?

○ Have I talked my plans over with my banker?

○ Have I talked my plans over with my lawyer?

○ Have I contacted the local Small Business Administration for SCORE/ACE counseling?

○ Have I done some library research on small business?

What About a Partner?

○ If I have, or plan to have, a partner, will that partner be providing something I couldn't provide alone?

○ Is the partner someone I can really get along with—even if times get tough?

○ Have I checked out the advantages and disadvantages of having (and being) a partner?

○ Has my lawyer checked out my partnership agreement?

ily; three quarters are married; half started a business because they disliked working for others.

Staying within a field of expertise increases chances for success. So does sales experience; as Chapter 11 discusses, salesmanship is part of any business—retail, wholesale, or manufacturing.

As for personality, try checking yourself out on the Entrepreneurial Personality Worksheet at the end of this chapter. This worksheet is based on one developed by the U.S. Small Business Administration (SBA) as part of their *Checklist for Going into Business*. Also, consider the following:

Do I Have an "I-Can-Do-It" Attitude?

Successful entrepreneurs have an "I-can-do-it" attitude. They are optimistic, not in the sense of just hoping for the best,

ENTREPRENEURIAL PERSONALITY WORKSHEET

Under each question, check the answer that says what you feel or comes closest to it. Be honest with yourself.

Are you a self-starter?

☐ I do things on my own. Nobody has to tell me to get going.

☐ If someone gets me started, I keep going all right.

☐ Easy does it. I don't put myself out until I have to.

Can you lead others?

☐ I can get most people to go along when I start something.

☐ I can give the orders if someone tells me what we should do.

☐ I let someone else get things moving. Then I go along if I feel like it.

Can you take responsibility?

☐ I like to take charge of things and see them through.

☐ I'll take over if I have to, but I'd rather let someone else be responsible.

☐ There's always some eager beaver around wanting to show how smart he is. I say let him.

How do you feel about other people?

☐ I like people. I can get along with just about anybody.

☐ I have plenty of friends—I don't need anyone else.

☐ Most people irritate me.

How good an organizer are you?

☐ I like to have a plan before I start. I'm ususally the one to get things lined up when the group wants to do something.

☐ I do all right unless things get too confused. Then I quit.

☐ You get all set and then something comes along and presents too many problems. So I just take things as they come.

How good a worker are you?

☐ I can keep going as long as I need to. I don't mind working hard for something I want.

☐ I'll work hard for a while, but when I've had enough, that's it.

☐ I can't see that hard work gets you anywhere.

but in believing in their capacity to make the best happen. A positive self-image and a belief in one's own potential are crucial to business success.

Do I Believe in Making My Own "Luck"?

Successful businesspeople don't trust to luck for their opportunities or blame fate for their failures. They don't wait for their ship to come in—they go out and launch a few. Luck and timing do influence the course of any business, but the true entrepreneurial personality tends to believe that "in every problem there is an opportunity," that luck is more a matter of identifying and seizing chances than waiting for windfalls.

Do I Have a Need to Achieve?

Not everyone has the same amount of ambition, motivation, or drive. Successful businesspeople have a high degree of all three. Their high need to achieve means that they are not satisfied with past successes.

Do I See Security As Residing in Myself or in Others?

This issue is known in psychological terms as one's **locus of security.** People whose locus of security rests outside themselves are more comfortable with a steady paycheck and without the need to make risky decisions themselves. The prospect of an income that rises and falls with the seasons or with business cycles makes them uneasy. Recent economic events indicate that even the steadiest job in a long-established industry may be less secure than it appears; nevertheless, the risks of an income dependent entirely on oneself are readily apparent. If you would rather trust yourself than others—any others—you may find that having your own business and making your own decisions actually increases your perception of security. Your locus of security is internal.

Other attributes that are essential to small-business success include get-up-and-go, perseverance, self-discipline, good organizational skills, decision-making ability, and, not least of all, good health.

CHAPTER TWO

Choosing the Right Business

KEY TERMS

cooperative
corporation
franchise
joint and several liability

joint venture
limited partnership
mutual company
nonprofit corporation

partnership
sole proprietorship
stockholder
syndicate
trust

What kind of business will be right for you? Maybe you already have an idea for a business based on your special knowledge, skill, experience, or interests. Even if you do, you may want to fine-tune your idea after you read this chapter. Maybe you know you'd like to start a business, but you're still looking around for ideas. Start with the ideas in this chapter, then look around at your community and the people in it. What do they need that you can supply? Remember that, in the end, success depends on providing something your po-

tential customers will want to buy *from you*.

Some General Rules

Take a look at the box, Business Ideas from A to Z. Long as it is, this list can't begin to encompass all the possibilities. What it can do is start you thinking. Highlight the ideas that appeal to you—or cross out those that don't. Some general rules may help you narrow down the possibilities.

BUSINESS IDEAS FROM A TO Z

Accounting service
Advertising agency
Antiques
Art supplies or lessons
Apparel (new or used)
Athletic clothing or supplies
Auto painting
Auto parking
Auto parts
Auto repairs
Auto sales

Baby-sitting
Bakery
Bar
Bartering service
Beauty shop
Bicycle shop
Bookkeeping service
Boutique
Burglar alarm

Camera store
Candle shop
Carpet cleaning
Car rental
Carwash
Catering
Ceiling fans
Child care
Chimney sweeping
Coin-machine route
Computer consulting
Computer sales or service
Consulting
Cookie vending
Cookware
Copy shop

Cosmetics
Craft supplies

Dance studio
Dating service
Disco
Dry cleaning

Editing or production service
Electronic supplies
Employment service

Fabric shop
Fish store
Fitness club
Fried-chicken takeout
Furniture rental

Game room
Garden supplies
Gifts
Graphics service

Hobby supplies
Housecleaning service

Ice-cream store
Import/export

Jewelry store

Kitchen remodeling

Landscape design
Landscape planting or maintenance
Lawn care

Mail order
Men's clothing

Microwave lessons
Mopeds
Music

Newsletter publisher

One-hour anything (photo, cleaner)

Paint and wallpaper
Paperback exchange
Pet grooming or pet sitting
Photocopying
Pizza shop
Popcorn shop
Portrait studio
Printing
Publicity agency

Racquetball club
Résumé service

Sailboat rentals
Secretarial service
Seminars
Service station
Solar energy

Stuffed-toys store

T-shirt store
Tavern
Telephone answering
Telephone sales
Theatrical booking
Tobacco shop
Travel agency

Vending machines
Video rentals
Videotaping

Warehouse
Watch repair
Waterbeds
Wedding gowns
Weight-loss clinic
Window cleaning
Word processing

Xylophone lessons

Yoga lessons

Zither store

Rule 1: Choose a Business You Know

Your chances of success increase greatly if you choose a business in which you've had previous experience or training. This rule may seem limiting, but it really isn't. You need not do *exactly* what you have done before: A hairdresser may open a cosmetics boutique; a secretary may start a word processing service; an athlete may start a sporting-goods store or a fitness center; a baker may start a catering service. The trick is to pick a field in which you have an interest, contacts, a sense of the tricks of the trade—but one that's different enough from what you were doing to keep you interested or to supply or anticipate a need.

Rule 2: Remember That Business Has Cycles

General economic conditions that you can't control may have good or bad effects on your business. During the fuel shortage, people traveled less. Travel-related business suffered. Gasoline and motel sales went down, but more dollars were spent on home repairs and landscaping supplies. When mortgage interest rates zoomed, new construction declined, but more people fixed up their existing homes.

Consumer tastes have cycles, too. People will always need to eat, but today more people eat in restaurants or buy prepackaged and catered foods. Fewer people cook from scratch at home. At one time you could find half a dozen T-shirt booths at every mall; count them today.

Rule 3: Analyze Your Interests

If you can't keep your checkbook straight and tend to put off paying bills, it's unlikely you'll want to start an accounting service. Are you good with your hands, or good with people? Do you like noise, action, and crowds, or shun them? Are you better with words or with numbers? Do you like gadgets or do machines conspire against you? Maybe your friends have told you how good you are at something—a craft, or cooking, or writing letters. Be careful, though; cooking is only a small part of running a restaurant, for example. There's ordering food, planning, decorating, scheduling, promoting, supervising to be done. Maybe a takeout catering service would be nearer to what you'd really like to be doing.

Are you good with a camera and good with children and pets? Perhaps a specialized photography service is for you. If you're good at tennis *and* good with people, maybe you could promote tennis tournaments, run a pro shop, design tennis clothes, or—what? Don't be afraid to let your imagination roam. Who would have thought that hot air balloons had a future? Or that sailmaking would become a bigger business than it was in the days of clipper ships?

ENTREPRENEURIAL INNOVATORS: "CRAZY IDEAS" THAT WORKED

Omitting the "crazy" entrepreneurs who turned out to be geniuses, like the Wright brothers or Henry Ford, consider some "crazy ideas" that innovators have turned into businesses:

- Writing "personals" ads to order
- Renting advertising space on cows
- Booking "stripping gorillas" for parties
- Bottling and selling "waters of the world"
- Balloon rides
- "Rent-a-Plant" service
- Date reminder service (anniversaries, birthdays)
- "Cow," "cat," and "pig" boutiques
- Erotic chocolates

Three Basic Kinds of Business

Once you know the general area of your interests, consider that there are three ways you can serve consumer needs in that area: Making a product (manufacturing), selling a product (retail or wholesale sales), or providing a service. These are the three basic categories of business. Of course, these categories overlap, but if you analyze the businesses you know, you'll see that one category predominates. For example, a millworking company manufactures prehung doors; that's producing a product. The building supply sells them to contractors (wholesale) or to do-it-yourselfers (retail). That's sales. An insurance company insures the doors, as part of a whole house, against damage by fire. That's a service.

Similarly, a meat-packing company, a supermarket, and McDonald's are all involved with hamburgers in some way, but for the meat packing company, production is the main activity; for the supermarket, sales is the main activity. With McDonald's, classification is more complicated. Do they sell a product (hamburgers) or a service (cooking the hamburgers and providing a place to eat them)?

At one time, basic manufacturing was the main business of U.S. business. Today, service is rapidly becoming dominant. You may have heard "service" defined somewhat contemptuously as "burger-flipping." If you stop to think about it, though, service is involved in many large and profitable enterprises, including health care, real estate (realtors don't ordinarily build and stock houses; they act as brokers between buyers and sellers), stock brokerage, insurance, and such recent additions as computer programming and consulting.

Where might you fit in? A limousine service? Equipment rental? Formal clothes rental or Santa Claus suits? Pool maintenance? Computer repair? Closet consultant? Tutoring? A mobile auto repair?

Services are what busy people need done for them because they don't have the time to do it for themselves. It just takes a creative mind and some talent to come up with a brand-new business in the service line.

Franchising: A Ready-Made Image

Before starting out entirely on your own, you might give some thought to **franchising.** Under this system, you have access to a ready-made product or service, complete with image, logo, trade secrets, and national advertising. You pay the parent company an upfront fee and ongoing royalties for the use of its name, for various amounts of equipment, specialized supplies, and assistance with marketing and managing the business. Your initial fee depends somewhat on how well established the franchised product is (new ventures cost less but are also more risky) and on the amount of equipment needed to start.

The best-known franchises are probably fast-food enterprises, so it may surprise you to learn that over one third of all U.S. retail sales are made through franchised outlets. Besides national franchises, there are also local ones including hairdressing, pizza, and many other products and services. Think of Century 21 (real estate), Dollar Rent-a-Car, Lawn Doctor, Speedy Printing, and a host of others including dance studios, fitness centers, lube shops, and bookstores. Up-front costs range from $15,000 to $100,000 and more, plus whatever working capital you need. (We'll discuss working capital later in this book.)

A franchise with a well-known, well-established company is far less risky than starting out entirely on your own. But in return for the help of the parent company in selecting a site, training your workers, and setting up and advertising your business, you give up a considerable amount of independence. To maintain their hard-won image, most franchisers exert strict controls over their franchisees.

Forms of Business Ownership

While you're deciding what kind of business you want to start, you should also consider how to acquire it and what form of ownership is best for you.

How Do I Become a Business Owner?

Basically, there are three ways to acquire a business:

○ You can inherit one.
○ You can buy an existing business.
○ You can create a new one from the beginning.

Obviously, inheriting a business costs the least. Purchasing a business may be the most costly overall and will almost certainly involve the greatest initial investment. Both these situations have the benefit of providing you with going concerns, complete with customers, an established reputation, and a helpful history of accounting records. These advantages make the business more predictable and increase the chances of successful operation.

Creating a new firm offers the most unknowns and unexplored areas. With a going concern, you can readily find out the number of customers and the expense involved in serving them. With a not-yet-established business, you face an uncertain future. How long will it be before the business is viable? How long before it makes a profit or provides you with a living? Will it succeed at all? There are means of estimating all these factors, which we will discuss. Even so, the accuracy of your estimates will have to be tested in the marketplace; until that occurs, you are dealing with many unkowns.

Adoption of an existing business is the more conservative choice. Conceiving and giving birth to a new one is riskier for the novice entrepreneur.

What are the risks? Dun & Bradstreet, a firm that compiles many business statistics, and the U.S. Small Business Administration, which uses data from the Department of Commerce, agree on the odds. You have less than a 50 percent chance of succeeding. Or, to put it differently, you have more than a 50 percent chance of failing. Of all new businesses, 55 percent fail before completing their first five years of operation. Every year, 400,000 firms close down for every 600,000 that open.

A solid business plan will increase your chance of survival. Preparing such a plan is discussed in Chapter 3.

Should I Go It Alone?

When a business is owned entirely by one person, the business is called a **sole proprietorship.** If you choose this form of business ownership, everything belongs to you. You collect all the profits—and you bear the full amount of any losses. Except for the legitimate equity claims of your creditors (for example, the holders of equipment loans or mortgages), no other person may claim ownership of your business.

The March 1986 *President's Report to Congress on Small Business* stated that 77 percent of U.S. small businesses were sole proprietorships, making this by far the most popular form of doing business. It is also the most common way of starting out in a business.

As a sole proprietor, you make all the decisions and answer only to yourself. You can take quick action in business situations. You need not "check with the home office"—you *are* the home office. You need not wait until the policy committee meets—*you* make policy. You'll wear many hats—perhaps all the hats your business offers. As the owner of a small business, especially during its early months, it will be you who opens the doors in the morning and locks them at night; hires, supervises, and, if necessary, fires the staff; orders mechandise and supplies, unpacks them, and arranges the displays; waits on customers (including the irritable ones); takes phone calls; rings up sales, collects unpaid bills, and deposits the money; keeps the records; and all the many large and small duties that running a business involves.

You'll find yourself laughing at those (including, perhaps, yourself) who say that small business owners are "so lucky—they only have to work when they feel like it." You are likely to be working 70 to 80 hours a week and taking the bookkeeping home to do on Sundays. Studies show that people who own businesses work harder and longer than most employees do—but they also tend to derive higher levels of satisfaction from their work.

As a sole proprietor, you alone are responsible for paying the bills, meeting the payrolls, paying taxes on time, and getting the orders out and the work done. In slow seasons, and especially when you are starting out, you may have to forgo your own salary to meet your expenses or loan payments. You may find yourself pouring your savings into the business to keep it going.

A sole proprietor has unlimited financial liability not only for all bills incurred by the business but for any lawsuits that might arise. Your house, your car, your personal savings may all be seized by creditors.

This total responsibility is really the only requirement for becoming a sole proprietor. Just by doing business on your own you automatically become the proprietor of that business. Of course, there are legal and tax requirements associated with doing business; these are discussed in Chapter 3.

Should I Take on a Partner to Share the Work?

A **partnership** is an association of two or more people who agree to share ownership of a business. Although a minimum of two people is required for a partnership, some businesses have several hundred partners.

You can start a partnership with a simple oral arrgement: "Let's do it!" It is wise, though, to put your partnership in writing and to consider its terms carefully before you do. Sample partnership agreements can be found in libraries. An attorney can write up a clear agreement for you, and this is advisable for any serious partnership. You will be sharing decisions, costs, profits, and losses with your partner. Your written agreement should state clearly:

○ The exact duties of each partner
○ The amount of time each will devote to the business
○ The division of profits
○ The terms under which either can withdraw from the business

---

STAN'S HONEYMOON WAS OVER

"We're friends, aren't we?" asked Len. "We can trust each other." Stan believed him; after all, Len had been his mentor in the health food business. Stan and Len formed a partnership to start a branch of their distributorship. Under their agreement, everything was to be 50-50—bank accounts, profits, and decisions.

The two partners soon found out how different their concepts of the business were. Stan had a "make-do" approach—used equipment, an old truck, fruit crates for shelving. Len wanted to start with a splash. "We're selling health, right? Our trucks should shine!"

Every day seemed to bring a new dispute. Then Stan left for his honeymoon. After two weeks in Bermuda he came back to find that Len had cleaned out the bank account and taken off for California in one of the new trucks—leaving Stan with the equipment loans to pay off and a number of angry customers whose deliveries had been skipped.

Stan's lawyer had suggested that two signatures be required on the checking account. Len had objected. "Who needs all that red tape?" Stan found out the answer to that when the honeymoon was over.

With a partnership arrangement you can share work, ideas, and profits. You can divide up the work according to expertise or preference. Perhaps one of you is the quiet, creative type, the other a born promoter. One may be better at management and finance, the other at selling. This kind of arrangement can have a number of benefits.

What a partnership does *not* do is divide up your liability to creditors or plaintiffs. In law, partners in a general partnership have what is called **joint and several liability.** This means that *each* partner is *fully liable* for the debts of the other(s). If one of you incurs financial commitments unwisely, the other may be held accountable for the debts. In the case of a lawsuit, the plaintiff can pursue any partner for the entire amount of the award. Each partner risks all his or her personal assets with unlimited liability. This unlimited liability aspect of partnership may explain why partnerships account for less than 7 percent of all U.S. businesses.

To avoid unlimited liability, a **limited partnership** may be formed. A limited partner restricts his or her liability to only those assets he or she had contributed to the business. These assets must be stipulated in writing and clearly defined. Lacking such an agreement, partners are subject to the unlimited liability described above.

Both partners may be equally active in a business, but variations also exist. A *silent partner* is known to the public but plays no active role in the enterprise. A *secret partner* is active but is not known to the public. A *dormant partner* is both silent and secret. A *nominal partner* lends the use of his or her name to the business—often because of personal fame—but is not active in the business and does not actually share in its ownership.

Should I Incorporate?

Forming a **corporation** creates a legal situation in which the assets of the businesses are separated from the assets of its owners. A corporation is "an artificial being, invisible, intangible, existing only in the contemplation of the law." The corporation, rather than its owners as individuals, owns cash and land belonging to the business, buys and sells, sues and is sued, and, if the business fails, goes bankrupt in its own name. The risks incurred by a corporation encompass only those assets that are in the business. Only those assets can be lost, and the liability of the owners is limited to them.

In the mid-1980s, 15 percent of U.S. businesses chose a corporate form of ownership. Most of these businesses are engaged in manufacturing, transportation, or other capital-intensive operations—those requiring very large investments in facilities and equipment. Although small in number, corporations earned 87 percent of all sales revenues in 1986. Their average profit on sales is low—just under 4 percent—but their volume of sales is enormous.

Huge corporations of this kind are usually publicly held—that is, their stock is sold to the general public. Small-business corporations are often closely held; their stock belongs to only those people who actually run the business, with token shares held by their attorneys.

The corporate structure consists of a board of directors, a chief executive (CEO) or president, and the owners—called shareholders, **stockholders,** or investors. The president or CEO, who actually runs the company, is chosen by the board of directors. This form of organization tends to have a longer life than a proprietorship or a partnership, since the board can employ a new operating officer in case of death or retirement. Corporations can grow larger than proprietorships and partnerships, and they have the advantage of being able to raise capital by the sale of stocks and bonds.

Investors provide the equity financing (capital) of the business by purchasing shares of stock, which entitle them to shares of the profits in the form of dividends. Stocks are not debts of the corporation—that is, they are not a claim against assets. Bonds, which are a form of borrowing rather than a form of ownership, are claims against the corporation.

The laws related to corporations differ from state to state. Federal laws governing corporations also exist. Both the state and federal governments treat a corporation as a separate "person"; it is taxed separately from its owners and must file and pay its own federal and state income tax returns. The profits remaining after taxes are distributed to the owners (stockholders), who must declare this income and pay federal, state, and sometimes local taxes on it.

Should you incorporate? If you decide to do so, see Chapter 3 for the beginning steps in doing so. A corporate structure may appeal to you because it appears to reduce your personal liability risk, or because it seems prestigious. It is true that a corporation will legally separate your assets from those of the business, but the price for doing this is high. You will pay additional state and federal taxes for the privilege; you will incur legal fees; your bookkeeping will be more complex and expensive; and you may find bankers hesitant to lend you start-up funds, since your personal assets are no longer backing up the business and your enterprise has no track record of profitability or even survival.

Instead, consider purchasing insurance to protect your personal assets from business risks. You can always incorporate later, when the business has become better established and its survival is more certain. Unless your business will earn $50,000 or so in profit, incorporation is likely to cost you more than a proprietorship or a partnership would. One exception would be a business that has a high and uninsurable risk of being sued and an owner with substantial wealth that only incorporation can protect. The other exception would be a business that is applying for nonprofit status.

Nonprofit corporations are not organized for the purpose of making a profit but for some charitable, cultural, educational, or community endeavor. Employees of nonprofit corporations may draw salaries, but the corporation distributes no profit in the form of dividends to stockholders. Nonprofit corporations have tax-exempt status under special state and federal rules. This book, however, assumes that you intend that your small business will be a profit-making enterprise.

There are other, specialized forms of corporations, some of which have arisen in response to tax laws. For example, Subchapter S of the Internal Revenue Code permits corporations that have fewer than a specified number of stockholders (currently 35) to elect to be taxed as partnerships. This rule enables relatively small firms to retain the corporate advantage of limited legal liability while avoiding the double taxation levied on corporations. Since tax laws continually change, you should consult a tax attorney or an accountant to determine current regulations.

Are There Other Forms of Ownership?

Although there are other forms of ownership, they are rarely used in small business. A **syndicate** is formed by pooling money for business purposes. Syndicates are legal if formed for a legal purpose, but the term has come to have a racketeering connotation. A **trust** is a form of organization in which designated persons manage the assets of a beneficiary—for example, for a child or for someone who cannot manage the property for some reason. A **joint venture** is a kind of short-term partnership in which two or more businesses join forces to accomplish a specified business objective. For example, a real estate firm may join with a building contractor and a financial institution to build a condominium or a shopping center with the intention of selling it as soon as it is ready for occupancy. When the objective has been completed, the joint venture dissolves. Like the other structures described here, the joint venture is rare in small business.

A **cooperative** is a business established and owned by its customers. For example,

a group of farmers who could not individually afford a grain storage facility may form a cooperative to own and operate it. Some well-known businesses are cooperatives, among them the Wakefern central buying facility of Shop-Rite supermarkets and the Ocean Spray cranberry marketing cooperative. This form is uncommon for small business.

In a **mutual company,** investors pool money for specific investment objectives. Mutual companies are involved in money markets, stocks, bonds, and precious metals trading. This form of organization is fairly common among insurance companies but rare in small business.

The Step-by-Step Route

Most businesses start as proprietorships. Later, if there is need for cash or talent that only a partner could provide, the firm may become a partnership. If the firm survives its early years and prospers, the next step may be incorporation. This enables the firm to acquire additional equity capital through the sale of stock to family and close friends. If further growth warrants the move, stock may be offered to the general public. A prospectus must be prepared, and the approval of the Securities and Exchange Commission must be obtained. These steps require the services not only of an accountant and an attorney but also of an investment broker.

A valuable source of information about incorporation—including timing, feasibility, and where to find an attorney or an accountant—are the U.S. Small Business Administration's SCORE/ACE chapters. More information about the SBA and its services can be found in Chapter 4.

CHAPTER THREE

Developing Your Business Plan

KEY TERMS

business plan
market potential

nondisclosure statement
sales potential

A "tag line" on the tea bags distributed by a well-known tea company says, "If you don't know what you want to do, it's harder to do it." Getting off to a good start with your new enterprise means knowing what you want to do, not in general terms, but clearly and specifically, and then making a business plan with clear, specific steps for doing it. Your plan should be in writing, and you should expect to spend a good deal of time—weeks or even months—putting your plan together before you take any action. Most business beginners underestimate both the importance of planning and the time it takes.

After you have developed a general plan for your business, you can begin making financial plans as described in Chapter 4. You'll want to choose a name for your business and consider the image you want it to project. But first you need to ask yourself, and possibly your potential customers, some searching questions.

What Business Will I Really Be In?

Maybe you think you've already answered that question. You're going to be in "the carpentry business." That kind of answer is at once too narrow and too broad. Maybe what you mean by carpentry is really building houses. If that's the case, you may find yourself adding plumbing, electrical work, insulating, heating—any number of services to your business. On the other hand, that may be more than you want to get into. Maybe what you meant by carpentry was building kitchen cabinets, or remodeling and restoring old homes.

"Building houses" is somewhat broad, even if building an entire home is what you had in mind. Maybe you've spotted a need for well-constructed small homes designed for retired people. Or for roomy but simple homes for young people with children. Or vacation homes. Or even assembling prebuilt homes. Only a very large construction firm would be likely to attempt such a wide range of projects—not to speak of industrial or commercial construction. You're better off specializing.

Again, if you think of your business as "candymaking" or "a florist shop," you're depriving yourself of opportunities for expansion. A candymaking enterprise, viewed from a broader perspective, is really in the business of selling gifts and impulse snacks. What about gift tie-ins to Valentine's Day, Easter, Mother's Day, or Christmas? Should you sell decorative tins? Trays? Stuffed animals? On the other hand, "candy" is a broad category. Perhaps you want to confine your business to making expensive gourmet candies, or hard candies shaped to a theme.

Your own belief about what business you're in will affect your business decisions. If you think of yourself strictly as a florist, are you likely to branch out into wedding design? Only taking a broad view and then narrowing down your choices within that broad perspective can you target a business that's exactly right for

you—and one that leaves you room for expansion.

Once you decide what business you're really in, write it down. Define it carefully. Include every activity and product your definition applies to. Then submit your idea to some veteran business owners. Listen to what they say. Then refine your definition again. Once you've done that, you'll be in a better position to estimate your customer base and to plan the steps that translate your business from idea to reality.

How Many Customers Can I Count On?

To decide whether your business is feasible, you'll need to estimate how many customers you're likely to have. Even businesses that supply universal needs like food can't expect to serve every customer in their trading area. How do you estimate your market potential (the total number of potential customers) and your sales potential (the number who will actually buy your product or service)? Marketing techniques are discussed in more detail in Chapter 9. For now, you need to work out a rough estimate of your potential sales volume.

What Is My Potential Trading Area?

How big is the area from which you expect to draw customers? For a mail-order business, the area may consist of the entire country, provided you advertise nationally. For a convenience grocery store, the trading area would be much smaller. Is

HOW CAN I PROTECT MY IDEA?

Do you have a great idea for a business? Has it remained just that—an idea—for years? Perhaps you lack money to put your idea into action. And perhaps one reason you lack money is that you are afraid to submit your idea to potential investors for fear it will be stolen. Or perhaps you have hesitantly revealed the idea to someone who has then put it into action himself—ignoring you.

At that point you can do nothing. You gave the idea away freely. An idea is not property; you *cannot patent an idea*. There is a means of protecting ideas, though; it's called a **nondisclosure statement.** Such a statement must be signed by the other party *before* you reveal your idea if it is to protect you.

You can find examples of nondisclosure statements at your library, or a lawyer can draw one up for you. Briefly, such documents state:

○ That you are the originator of the disclosed invention
○ That the other party has not thought of such an idea
○ That he or she will not use the idea without your permission
○ That he or she will not reveal your idea to anyone else
○ That he or she will regard your idea as highly confidential

You must also write to the Commissioner of Patents, Washington, D.C. 20231, stating that you are the originator of the invention you describe and that you request that the attached description of the idea be accepted under the Disclosure Document Program and preserved for a period of two years. The Patent Office will assign a Disclosure Document number.

While you are developing your idea, you should preserve all notes and maintain memoranda to show dates, steps you have taken, projects you have completed, research, plans, funds expended, persons contacted, and efforts made. Should someone take your idea in violation of a nondisclosure statement, these records may establish you as the originator of the idea.

These procedures give you the maximum protection possible from having your ideas used by others while you are seeking investors, partners, and associates.

your area a neighborhood? A town or city? A state or region? Don't guess the population; get current, actual figures. Your local Chamber of Commerce can help.

Not every age group or economic group is likely to buy your product or service. Suppose you decide to start an aquatic sports business. What age group buys surfboards? Scuba equipment? Rafts? Suppose that it is teenagers who buy surfboards. What is the teenage population in your area? And what percentage of those teenagers are in families affluent enough to support a surfing hobby? Those teenagers constitute your **market potential.**

Now, be realistic. Even among teens who can afford them, not all will buy a surfboard. Estimate how many already have bought surfboards. Are 10 percent of the remainder likely to buy one? Those 10 percent constitute your **sales potential.**

You can use the same procedure for any business, although some estimates will be firmer than others. If you want to start an auto painting business, start with motor vehicle registration figures. You might decide that owners of cars eight to twelve years old are potential customers—and so on.

Not Everyone Will Buy from You

Your enthusiasm about your business is likely to distort your view of demand for your products and services. "Everyone needs my widget" is a common misconception. Some people may decide they don't need widgets. Some may never hear of them despite your best marketing efforts. Some may not be able to afford one. Not every owner of a rusty car will have it painted. (Those who don't might be potential customers for a DON'T LAUGH—IT'S PAID FOR bumper sticker, though.)

Try to estimate how many people will buy from you in a year. For example, if about 1,000 babies are born in your trading area in a year, and most people buy two pairs of shoes for an infant in its first year, the total potential sales for the year are 2,000 pairs of shoes. You'll have to divide that by the number of businesses that sell baby shoes in your area. Perhaps there are only three; yours would be the fourth. That means your maximum sales potential might be 500 pairs of shoes. (Some people will buy by mail order, some people will use hand-me-downs, and so on. You may want to deduct a safety margin.)

Now, to determine your maximum dollar sales volume, multiply 500 by the average cost of a pair of baby shoes. That's your anticipated gross income (not profit) for a year. You can estimate the weekly gross by dividing by 52; remember, though, that sales volume fluctuates seasonally.

Before you reach conclusions about demand (how many people will want what you offer), take a look at the competition. Leaf through the Yellow Pages. Drive through the business district. Go to the library and look at newspaper ads for the past year—and for a few years ago. If there are many competing businesses, or if the number of competitors is rising fast, the market may be overcrowded. On the other hand, having *no* competition may not be a good sign either. Has someone tried your kind of business and failed? If so, why?

Population Trends Make a Difference

You also need to examine trends. Is the number of customers expanding or shrinking? Some communities are losing population; others are gaining. If shopping malls ring the city, or if it appears that they soon will, locating in the center of town may be inadvisable.

But there's more to it than that. If your community is growing, who is moving in? Families with children? Young professionals? Retired people? Suppose you want to sell swimming pools. Growth in the first two categories might be advantageous for you; the third might not.

Try to find out how well your potential competitors are doing. A trade association might be able to tell you the number of sales per business. A trade organization or publication may also possess figures on the size of population needed to support a given type of business, or how much sales volume a town of a given size can generate. For example, the National Association of Dry Cleaners formerly estimated that it takes a population of 10,000 to support one dry-cleaning establishment. Opening a dry-cleaning shop in a town of 50,000 with seven existing shops would be unwise.

Location . . . Location . . . and Location

With the exception of deciding what business you'll be in, "Where Should I Locate?" is the single most important question you should answer. There's an old saying that only three considerations matter when you buy real estate: location, location, and location. The saying applies to your business, too, not only for a retail store but for any kind of small business enterprise. Since people become accustomed to finding you in a certain place, it's important to make sure that your initial location is a good one. It should serve you for at least the first five years.

It's natural to think of starting out in your home town, but is that the best choice? Who lives there? What is the income level? The age level? What kinds of homes do people have? Does your business serve customers in their leisure hours, or does it serve other businesses? Avoid the common pitfall of assuming that where you are now is where your business should be.

Keep Your Customers in Mind

If you live in Basalt, Idaho, and you want to start a bagel bakery—stop and think. How many Basalters eat bagels now? Is there a ready-made market, or will you have to introduce bagels to the local population and hope enough people like them (or will even try them) to support your bakery?

Cultural, religious, and ethnic variety is part of the wonderful diversity of America. But cultural and ethnic groups are not distributed uniformly across the United States or even within states. There are Irish, German, Polish, Greek, Hispanic, Arabic, Scandinavian, and Italian enclaves in different cities, states, and regions. Each group has favorite food choices, religious observances, and cultural habits. What is beautiful to one group may seem boring or garish to another. What one group finds delicious may be distasteful to another. What seems conservative in one place may seem outlandish in another. And some populations—often in large cities—are more ready to try something new than others are.

Since Americans are so different from one another, you need to select an area with a high concentration of your potential customer group in mind. To ignore ethnic and cultural differences could greatly lengthen the time you need to get established; it could even jeopardize the survival of your business.

Do Your Homework

"Everyone eats out," you may think when you decide to start a restaurant. But while in some cities people eat as many as ten meals a week out, in others people eat as few as four meals out. Some people eat everyday meals out; others eat out only on special occasions. The kind of food they choose varies, too. For example, you might think of pizza as being more American than Italian—a food "everybody" eats. But in a Pennsylvania city of 50,000, the owner of the only pizza shop in town retired in the early 1980s after 20 years in the business—and only the prior year had he been doing any significant volume of business. Local citizens, he said, found pizza too exotic to try.

In cities with a high proportion of clerical and managerial workers, dress shirts and dry cleaning will sell better than in a city with a high proportion of blue-collar workers. A coin laundry will do better in a city with many apartment dwellers. Luxury items sell better in high-income areas, but consumer loan businesses are apt to do better elsewhere.

To find out about the communities where you are thinking of locating, do some research. Your local Chamber of Commerce can probably help. At your library, check out the *Statistical Abstracts of the United States*. This annual publication of the U.S. Census Bureau has ample information on population density, population growth, incomes, occupations, and similar data.

Sales and Marketing Management magazine, published in New York City, produces an annual survey of buying power, which compares purchasing patterns in major U.S. cities for such items as hardware, furniture, and automotive products. You should also check the annual *Gale Directory of Publications*, available at libraries, for the names of trade and industrial publications related to the business you are contemplating. These may give you the information you seek or suggest where you can find it. Trade publications and trade associations are good sources for such information as how much population is required to support a particular kind of business.

Don't forget to glance through the local newpapers, especially if you are investigating an area that's new to you. Major highway construction, the pattern of public transportation, development plans—all can affect your business for good or bad. A major new industry may mean more customers; a plant shutdown may mean fewer.

THE SINKING OF SALLY'S SUB SHOP

Almost from the beginning, Sally's Sub Shop was a big success. Her secret was in the rolls—they were crisp and fresh, while other shops in town used rolls that were often soggy and stale. Also, Sally started her business on a busy highway leading back to town from an amusement park and close to a women's college and two office parks. The only problem was the nearby intersection, where there were mile-long backups at busy times.

When Sally had been in business for three years and was thinking of establishing a branch, the state built a bypass to relieve the congested intersection. Instead of two-way traffic past her doors, she had one-way traffic only—leading *out* of town. To get to her shop from the college or the office park, customers had to negotiate a long, confusing jughandle and three traffic lights. "We can't get there from here!" her customers wailed. Sally's business dropped by half, then two-thirds.

Bad luck? The bypass had been mapped out for several years before Sally started her business. The local paper had carried more than a dozen articles about it, showing the proposed traffic patterns. Sally hadn't checked them. Not bad luck but poor planning sank Sally's Subs.

Your Product or Service Affects Your Location

If you sell lawnmowers, swimming pools, or outdoor carpeting, apartment renters are not potential customers for you—and condominium owners may not be good customers either. Toys or children's clothes may not sell well in an area where many senior citizens live, unless your niche is selling specialty items to doting grandparents. A "bedroom" community whose residents work in another city may be a poor choice for a photocopy shop, since people are likely to do their photocopying where they work.

Are you selling impulse items? Commercial or industrial goods? Specialty items? To sell impulse items, you need to have lots of people passing by where they can see, smell, and touch. (A very high-volume street or corner may actually be a poor location for this kind of shop because traffic is too fast or too frantic.) A service business such as auto repair may not require a high-population neighborhood, and a service business that makes house calls needs to consider not traffic past the business but travel time to customers' homes or offices.

If your product or service is very specialized—replacement parts for photocopiers, printers' inks, and so on—customers may come to you even in an out-of-the-way, low-rent location. If you are selling a luxury product, however, you need a location where customers feel safe about walking or leaving their cars.

Competition May Help You Sell

Being near the competition may be an advantage or a disadvantage. Car dealers, furniture stores, and other sellers of high-ticket items often locate close to one another. Customers buy these things infrequently; they like to take their time— looking around, shopping prices, comparing features. Don't be all alone if you are selling items like this; an "auto mile" or a concentration of furniture stores will draw more potential customers into your orbit.

Ten Points to Consider When You Choose a Location

Apart from general rules and cautions regarding location, there are ten specific points to keep in mind—especially for a retail business. Some have already been discussed, and some are discussed below.

1. Locate near a sufficient number of potential customers.
2. Locate near compatible businesses.
3. Provide abundant free parking.
4. Provide easy access and egress.
5. Consider traffic patterns.
6. Locate among prosperous businesses.
7. Make sure your business is easy to find.
8. Choose an area with a suitable demographic profile.
9. Avoid blighted locations.
10. Consider the time, the season, and the economy.

Parking. Fewer and fewer people go shopping on foot. With a few big-city ex-

ceptions, public transportation is also declining. For the foreseeable future, the automobile is Americans' chosen way of getting where they want to go. Convenient free parking is mandatory for any retail business today.

Ease of Access. In considering parking you also need to consider making it easy for people to get from the street or highway into the parking area and from the parking area into your place of business. Is the parking lot entrance clearly visible? Can people get to it without crossing traffic? If the parking lot is at the rear of your business, is the rear entrance attractive and clearly marked? Don't forget access for customers in wheelchairs or who are otherwise impeded.

Street Traffic Patterns. Not all streets are equal in the traffic they carry, and both sides of a two-way street are not necessarily equal in terms of your business. Try to locate on the side of the street carrying traffic appropriate to what you are selling. A breakfast-oriented business should be on the "to work" side; perishables like ice cream or cut flowers will sell better on the "homegoing" side.

Besides commuting traffic, streets carry people to other destinations that may also affect sales. You'll sell more bait and tackle on the side approaching a lake; refreshments may sell better on the homegoing side.

A one-way street carrying a heavy volume of traffic in the wrong direction (wrong for you) can be a serious impediment to your business. If you do locate on a one-way street, consider that in the United States, people prefer to park on the right side of the street. All other factors being equal, you'll do more business if you're on that side.

Climate makes a difference, too: The shady side of the street or a tree-lined street will be more appealing in hot weather. Some streets channel the wind in winter; pedestrians may shun them for that reason.

Seeking Prosperity. Check out the street you are considering. Current merchandise, clean windows with current displays, well-kept storefronts, and ample pedestrian traffic are good signs. Dusty show windows, out-of-date merchandise, and few customers shold give you pause. Do you really want to take the chance that your one new business will revitalize the neighborhood? If the neighborhood is deteriorating, and if existing businesses with established reputations can't succeed there, it's unrealistic to believe that you can.

Visibility. Can approaching customers see your business? Try driving past the location. Then try walking. Does a hedge, a tree, or a protruding building block the view? Can your location be seen from several angles and at a reasonable distance considering the speed of traffic? Being set back from the line of buildings or from the road can make the building more attractive but less visible.

Consider local landmarks, too. Being able to advertise your business as "across from the post office" or "on the square" is an advantage.

Avoiding Blight. Have you ever noticed that some leased locations seem to be the "touch of death"? Business after business opens and then quickly closes. Restaurants seem especially vulnerable to this pattern, and local people are usually well aware of these locations. The tipoff is one "Under New Management" sign after another. Try to avoid having to battle public knowledge of previous failure.

Time, Season, and Economics. Some businesses are seasonal; others are cyclical. Timing of the opening is crucial for businesses that are seasonal: opening an income tax service in June guarantees a long wait for customers; so does opening a swimming pool supply business in November.

Compatibility. Certain businesses are helped by having certain neighbors. For example, a drugstore and a supermarket can reinforce each other's business, whereas neither a dentist nor an auto body shop would benefit from proximity.

Customers are in certain buying moods at particular times. They tend not to mix spending trips. Going to the bank seems to fit in with going to the post office or library, but not with shopping for carpet. On the other hand, shopping for carpet seems to mix well with shopping for furniture, paint, and wallcovering, or even hardware. Shopping for a dress and for groceries are not compatible activities; on the other hand, shopping for shoes, handbags, or even cosmetics blends well with shopping for clothes. If you observe shopping areas carefully, you'll see that those with well-integrated offerings seem to prosper; those with a patchwork of dissimilar businesses often have marginal tenants who come and go quickly.

Avoid incompatible business neighbors. They cannot help your business and may harm it. We rarely look for an auto differential, an azalea, and a bottle of gin on the same shopping trip.

As a final precaution, use the Business Location Checklist (see box).

BUSINESS LOCATION CHECKLIST

About the Area in General:

○ Would a city or the suburbs be a better location?

○ Which city or region under consideration has the most potential customers for my product or service?

○ Which is better for me: a downtown location or a shopping center?

○ Is a residential, commercial, or industrial area best?

○ Are the income and lifestyle of the population suited to what I'm selling?

○ How many competitors do I already have? Have I used the Yellow Pages to plot my competitors on a city map?

○ What advantage over my competitors does my location give me? What advantages over me does it give them?

○ Is there enough parking?

○ Do competing businesses look prosperous?

○ Who will be my strongest competitor? What can I do to gain the advantage over that competitor?

About a Specific Neighborhood or Building:

○ Is the neighborhood improving or running down?

○ Have I checked planning board, zoning, and highway department records for potential changes such as throughways, major developments, one-way streets?

○ Is there adequate street traffic all day? Is traffic so heavy that drivers can't enter or exit?

○ Do pedestrians look like potential customers?

○ Is street lighting adequate for safety and to prevent vandalism?

○ Will the landlord provide snow removal? Structural repairs?

○ What are the lease terms? Can I secure a five-year lease? What are the terms for canceling the lease?

Additional questions related to location involve such matters as zoning and legal considerations.

Now that you have made some decisions about the kind of business you want, the customers you will serve, and the location you will choose, it is time to put your business plan in writing.

Formulating Your General Business Plan

Writing things down will help you clarify your thoughts. You will also be able to evaluate any gaps or contradictions in your planning. When the time comes to seek financing, your business plan will help convince potential lenders that you have given careful thought to your enterprise.

The business plan presented here is based on the *Business Planning Guide* developed by David H. Bangs, Jr., and his partner, Steve White (Dover, NJ: Upstart Publishing Company), and is reproduced with their permission.

Your **business plan** should consist of three main parts: a brief statement of purpose, the main body of the plan, and the supporting documents, as outlined below.

COVER SHEET: Name of business, name(s) or principal(s), address and phone number of business

STATEMENT OF PURPOSE:

I: The Business
A. Description of business
B. Product or service
C. Market
D. Competition
E. Location
F. Management
G. Personnel
H. Application and expected effect of loan (if you are applying for one)
I. Summary

II: Financial Data
A. Sources and applications of funds
B. Capital equipment list
C. Balance sheet
D. Break-even analysis
E. Income projections (profit and loss statement)
   1. Three-year summary
   2. Detail by month for first year
   3. Detail by quarter for second and third years
   4. Notes of explanation
F. Pro-forma cash flow
   1. Detail by month for first year
   2. Detail by quarter for second and third years
   3. Notes of explanation
G. Deviation analysis
H. Historical financial reports of existing business (if applicable)
   1. Balance sheets for past three years
   2. Income statements for past three years
   3. Tax returns

SUPPORTING
DOCUMENTS:

Personal résumés of principals; personal financial requirements and statements; cost-of-living budget; letters of reference; job descriptions; letters of intent; copies of leases, contracts, or legal documents; anything else of relevance to the plan.

Subsequent chapters in this book will help you in completing your business plan. This plan will not only provide you with valuable assistance in making final decisions about starting your business, it will also provide you with a road map to guide you through the precarious first three years.

CHAPTER FOUR

Developing Your Financial Plans

KEY TERMS

accounts payable

accounts receivable

assets

balance sheet

break-even analysis

cash flow projection

fixed costs

goodwill

hold harmless agreement

liabilities

net worth

operating costs

owner's equity

owner's investment

real property

variable costs

Your business plan sketched the broad outlines of your business operations. Now you need to translate your plans into dollars. When you have done so, some of the results will be incorporated into your business plan. You will also be taking care of certain details that occur no matter what business you select, and you will be looking for sources of assistance with your planning and with the actual start-up. These activities are discussed in Chapter 5.

Of course, you'll also be working on some of the preparations discussed under marketing, such as naming your business and deciding on how to promote and market it to customers. To make financial plans, you'll need a rough idea of such matters as whether you will have employees, and how many; what kind of advertising you will do; what you will spend on insurance, and so on. In fact, it may seem to you that you "can't do anything until you've done everything." It's best to read through the remainder of the chapters, then to come back and fill in the gaps in your financial plans. A computer is a big help in financial planning (see Chapter 6,

"The Computer and Your Business"); if you expect to buy one, consider doing it now so that it can help you in making your financial projections.

You will need several kinds of financial plans in order to estimate:

○ Your start-up expenses: your onetime cost of getting going
○ Your operating expenses (profit and loss)
○ Your cash flow
○ Your break-even point
○ The value of your ownership equity, or net worth

Calculating these estimates can be very complicated. It's best to have the assistance of an accountant, or at the very least to consult some specialized books on bookkeeping and accounting. The explanations in this chapter will give you an overview of the kind of information you will need.

Estimating Onetime Start-Up Costs

Use the start-up cost worksheet to estimate the expenditures you must make before you can start transacting business.

MY ESTIMATE OF START-UP COSTS

Licenses and permits	$ _____
Decorating and remodeling	_____
Fixtures (showcases, lighting, etc.)	_____
Equipment (include office equipment)	_____
Machinery	$ _____
Installation fees	_____
Lease deposits	_____
Utility deposits (electric, phone, heat)	_____
Starting inventory	_____
Legal fees, accounting fees	_____
Grand opening advertising/ promotion	_____
Operating cash	_____
Reserve for unexpected costs	_____
Other (list each item)	_____
TOTAL	$ _____

Be Sure to Include All Onetime Expenses

Some of the items in the worksheet are self-explanatory. Not all may apply to your particular business, but be sure to give each item careful thought before deciding that you can skip it. Some businesses do not require permits; others do. (Obtaining permits is discussed in Chapter 5.) Decorating and remodeling may consist of a few gallons of paint and considerable elbow grease (keep a record of the money you spend; it's part of your investment).

Fixtures—showcases, bookcases, work tables—may be simple or elaborate, depending on what you can afford and the image your business requires. For example, when Volkswagens were first sold in the United States, one dealer—who had started with a foreign-car repair shop—used the wooden crates in which parts were shipped for desks. Today that agency does several million dollars' worth of business annually.

When you consider equipment, don't neglect the little things: staplers, measuring tools—whatever your business requires. Machinery may or may not be necessary. Remember to allow for installation or, if you decide to lease some of your equipment, onetime deposits or leasing fees. Your utility company and the telephone company will probably require deposits from you as a new business, and if you and not a landlord are supplying heat, a first-time fill-up of the fuel tank must be paid for.

Even if you aren't selling goods at retail, you'll need a start-up inventory of every kind of supply, from paper clips to toilet tissue.

Onetime legal fees and accounting fees would include drawing up partnership or nondisclosure agreements, calculating tax strategies, and so on.

You'll be spending something on promotion, whether it's balloon flights for first-day customers or simply a mailing to potential clients and a few newspaper announcements. Promotion is discussed in Chapter 10; when you've made a list of strategies and estimated their costs, you'll be ready to fill in this item.

Don't forget that you'll need cash to operate. You'll always need some kind of floating cash fund, even when money starts coming in from customers. But in the beginning, cash for everyday expenses is a vital necessity.

JIM AND BEN ALMOST GOT SWAMPED

Jim and Ben had a well-thought-out plan for the 1930s apartment building they bought at auction. The spacious lobby, bronze stair rails, mosaic floors, and other Art Deco features would be almost impossible to duplicate at today's construction prices. The roomy apartments were perfectly laid out for offices, and the building's proximity to a small hospital promised professional tenants. Jim and Ben worked out a five-year plan for converting the apartments to offices as they became vacant. As it happened, they took possession of the building on October 1, the beginning of the heating season. The furnace worked fine—but there was no heat. Knots of angry tenants gathered in the hallways. After four expensive days, the problem was located and repaired. Everything the boiler had been producing had been leaking out beneath the building. To fix the leak, the heating crew was forced to jackhammer through the mosaic tile floors. Luckily, Jim and Ben had set aside a large cash fund for repairs. Had they not done so, their plans might have been swamped.

Do you have enough of your own cash to cover your start-up costs? If not, you should probably wait until you do. You'll need money to keep going during the first months or even the first year or two. It's unwise to be in debt before you start.

Be sure to keep careful records of all money of your own that you put into the business out of savings. This is called the **owner's investment.** Later, when money starts coming in regularly, you will be able to repay yourself. This repayment will be a *return of your owner's investment*—not income. To substantiate that it is not income, you must have proof of your expenditures. Save receipts now for future tax purposes.

What If I'm Buying an Existing Business?

Compare your start-up costs to the price being asked for any existing business you're thinking of buying. Subtract start-up costs from the asking price. Be sure to find out whether any inventory is included as part of the purchase price; if so, subtract this too. The difference is what you are paying for **goodwill**—the value of having established customers. You'll have to judge whether the nature of the business and its reputation justify the price. Remember that existing customers may not continue to patronize the business once you own it, but also remember that establishing a solid customer base is expensive.

In addition to inventory (stock of goods for sale or materials for production), you may also be buying **accounts receivable** (money owed *to* the business for credit purchases) and **accounts payable** (money owed *by* the business for credit purchases). Be sure that the sellers provide you with a signed list of accounts payable, together with a written agreement that they will pay any bills not included on the list.

Usually your attorney will be sure that all equipment, furniture, **real property** (buildings and grounds), and so forth are listed on the purchase contract. Make sure you understand what is and is not being included: Is the grandfather clock that makes the antique shop so inviting part of the stock, or is it the present owner's personal heirloom?

Sometimes you can buy a business—especially one that is in trouble—simply by agreeing to pay off the owner's existing debts. If you do this, have your attorney draw up a **hold harmless agreement** for the seller to sign. This agreement protects you from having to pay any unstated debts. The agreement should include pending lawsuits or claims. You don't want to find yourself buying liabilities you knew nothing about.

Does the purchase price include the building the business is in? Does it include the land? (Sometimes land is leased, even though a building is owned.) If the building is not included and the business is being conducted on leased premises, be careful to have your agreement list exactly what furniture, equipment, and fixtures are included and which belong to the landlord. (Lighting fixtures, as well as anything that is attached to the building such as gas stoves or plumbing fixtures, generally are the landlord's under the terms of the lease.) Make sure you can take over the existing lease or, if not, find out what a new lease will cost.

Does the business name transfer to you? If it is the registered property of the sellers, they may not permit you to use it. (This would affect the value of the goodwill.)

Estimating Your Operating Costs

Your **operating costs** are the day-to-day expenses of running your business. To estimate them accurately, you will first have to read the remaining chapters in this book. Some general notes and cautions are in order, however. Some of your operating costs will be relatively fixed—that is, you will incur them so long as you are in business, regardless of whether you have customers or not. Fixed costs include such items as rent, insurance, basic advertising, heat and light, property taxes, license fees, and so on.

Other costs fluctuate according to the volume of business. For example, if you are operating a restaurant, your costs for food, paper napkins, and so on will go up with the volume of business and will be lower when business is slow. Don't make the mistake, however, of thinking there will be *no* food costs during slow times. There is bound to be waste.

Wages might be called both fixed and fluctuating. Some staff (even if only yourself) will be needed no matter how slow business is. We will talk more about fixed versus flexible expenses in relation to calculating your break-even point (below).

In estimating your profit (or loss), begin by looking over the worksheet. This will give you an idea of the kinds of expenses you must anticipate. Later, when you have read the rest of this book, you can use the worksheet to create an estimated operating statement. Some 60 of the terms will be clearer to you then.

Prepare anticipated operating statements for several time periods: by the month, the quarter, and the year. For the early stages of your business, prepare monthly estimates. Expenses paid annually or quarterly should be divided by the appropriate number of months before being entered. You are virtually certain to arrive at a negative profit figure (a loss) for the early months.

"Sales" are the gross (total) receipts you get from customers, regardless of whether they are paid to you in cash or are billed. "Cost of goods sold" is just that: the total you have paid to suppliers for the goods or raw materials themselves. Remember that "Wages" should include a salary for yourself; otherwise your profit figure will not be a true profit. "Taxes and Licenses" includes taxes on the business, such as corporate taxes, as well as various employment taxes; it does not include your personal taxes on the salary you draw, or employees' taxes that you merely withhold from their wages for transmittal to the government. However, if you plan to pay such benefits as health insurance, life insurance, or vacation pay, you must include that in employee expenses.

First-time entrepreneurs tend to overestimate their sales volume for the first month and first year and underestimate their expenses. When you have completed your calculations, take another look. Reduce your sales estimate and increase your expense estimate; it's safer to underestimate your profits than to overestimate

ANTICIPATED MONTHLY OPERATING STATEMENT

TOTAL SALES $ _____
   Less Cost of Goods Sold   − _____
GROSS PROFIT   _____

EXPENSES
   Wages, salaries, benefits $ _____
   Rent for premises   _____
   Taxes and licenses   _____
   Advertising   _____
   Insurance   _____
   Telephone   _____
   Heat   _____
   Utilities: gas, electric,
     sewer, water   _____
   Maintenance, trash removal   _____
   Delivery and/or transportation   _____
   Supplies   _____
   Legal and accounting fees   _____
   Dues, subscriptions   _____
   Travel and entertainment   _____
   Office supplies, postage   _____
   Interest   _____
   Employee taxes: FICA,
     unemployment   _____
   Depreciation and/or
     equipment leases   _____
   Unclassified   _____

TOTAL EXPENSES   − $ _____

NET PROFIT BEFORE TAXES $ _____
   Less estimated local, state,
   and federal business taxes   − _____

NET PROFIT AFTER TAXES $ _____

TAXES ON YOUR BUSINESS

Many taxes are part of your fixed expenses. Check out which ones apply to you and count them into your financial plans. Taxes related to payroll are discussed in Chapter 8: "Organizing Your Small Business."

○ **State and Local Sales Taxes.** This is a tax that you collect on each sale of specified merchandise and transmit to the state or municipality. You will need a sales tax number, which is often the same as your federal identification number.

○ **Real Estate Taxes.** These taxes are part of your fixed expenses and are levied against the real property (land and buildings) of your business.

○ **Business Personal Property Taxes.** Some localities also tax business machinery, tools, and equipment.

○ **Sewer Taxes.** These are generally assessed on the basis of water usage. Sometimes they are based on the number of plumbing units on your premises. Some businesses are also assessed a tax by the Environmental Protection Agency (EPA).

○ **Registration Fees.** The municipality or county may require that your business be registered and that you pay a local fee. If you operate under a name other than your own (Acme Plumbing, for example), you must register under an assumed name regulation and possibly pay an additional fee.

○ **Licenses.** Your business may require a license and/or inspections: for example, restaurants and other food handlers must be licensed. So must plumbers, electrical contractors, auto salvage businesses, and real estate brokers and salespersons. Contact your state's department of economic development or your city's department of licenses and inspections.

○ **Special Taxes.** There are many special taxes. Some, like sales taxes, are simply collected from customers and transmitted to the state. Others must be paid by you. Check on beverage taxes, cigarette taxes, motorcarriers' road taxes, and so on. Your state department of commerce can provide a list.

Tax laws change. Use this checklist as a starting point, but don't assume that it is complete.

them. Methods for estimating sales volume are discussed below in relation to the break-even point.

Remember, too, that your business volume will ordinarily be lower in the early months than later. In any business, though, there are bound to be slow periods when cash accumulated during busy times must be drawn on to carry business costs. Since business in your early months is bound to be less than full volume, it helps to open your business just prior to a peak time.

Estimating Your Cash Flow

Besides estimating your profit, you need to make a month-by-month estimate of cash flow. A **cash flow projection** allows you to forecast the actual cash flowing into and out of your business over a given period. Cash outlays and expenses are not the same, and cash flow and profit analysis are not the same. It is possible to be making a profit yet to be short of cash, either because some of your sales are on credit, or because you must put out cash for expenditures that will later be amortized, such as equipment purchases. Start-up costs also affect cash flow rather than profit.

The Sample Cash Flow Worksheet below was provided by the U.S. Small Business Administration. Your accountant may have a similar form, or you can find one in texts on bookkeeping and account-

ing. When you make your estimated cash forecast, complete one for each month individually to allow for seasonal fluctuations.

Calculating Your Break-Even Point

Break-even analysis is an accounting tool that can take a great deal of the guesswork out of starting a venture, whether it is a whole new business, a branch or sideline, or an advertising or promotional venture. By using a mathematical formula based on your fixed and variable costs, you can determine either how many units (hours, service calls, products) you have to sell or how many dollars you have to take in order to break even—that is, to recover your expenses. Beyond the break-even point you are making a profit; below that point you are operating at a loss. You can calculate your break-even point by the day, the month, year, or for a specific activity.

As mentioned above, all business costs can be classified as being either fixed or variable. **Fixed costs** do not change as your business volume increases or decreases. For example, you have to pay rent, salaries, some insurance, and some utilities whether you are closed for vacation, open and doing little business, or having a flurry of sales. On the other hand, **variable costs** such as salepeople's commissions, shipping and delivery expenses, some wages, and the cost of goods sold increase when you are busy and decrease when your business is slow.

To figure your break-even point, you must first list your fixed and variable costs separately and total each list. Then determine the selling price for one item or service that you are selling. (If you sell a variety of services or products, you may need to do a separate calculation for each one, or you may use an average.)

Calculating Break-Even by Units Sold

Let BE = break-even point in units of products

FC = total fixed costs

SP = selling price of one unit

VC = total variable costs

Your formula is:

$$BE = \frac{FC}{SP - VC}$$

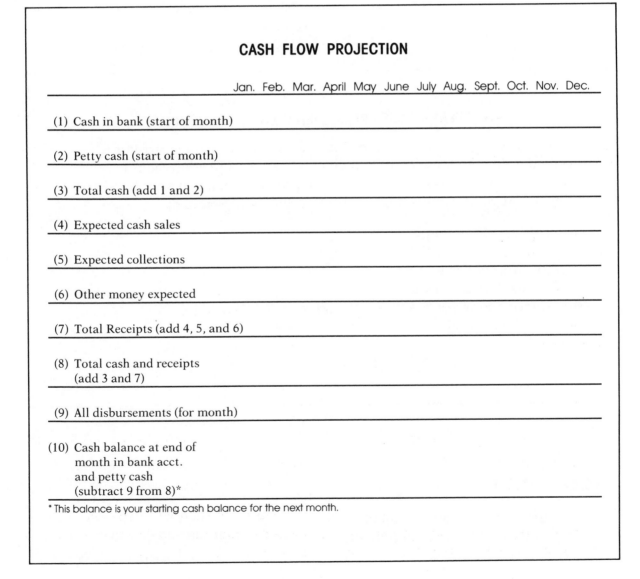

CASH FLOW PROJECTION

Jan. Feb. Mar. April May June July Aug. Sept. Oct. Nov. Dec.

(1) Cash in bank (start of month)

(2) Petty cash (start of month)

(3) Total cash (add 1 and 2)

(4) Expected cash sales

(5) Expected collections

(6) Other money expected

(7) Total Receipts (add 4, 5, and 6)

(8) Total cash and receipts
(add 3 and 7)

(9) All disbursements (for month)

(10) Cash balance at end of
month in bank acct.
and petty cash
(subtract 9 from 8)*

* This balance is your starting cash balance for the next month.

That is, *BE* is the number of units you must sell in order to break even. For example, suppose you were contemplating a $10,000 advertising campaign to sell shirts. The shirts cost you $15 each, and the selling price is $25. In this oversimplified example, there are no other costs. *SP* equals $25; *FC* equals $10,000; *VC* equals $15.

$$BE = \frac{\$10,000}{\$25 - \$10}$$

therefore

$$BE = \frac{\$10,000}{\$15}$$

therefore

$$BE = 1,000 \text{ shirts}$$

In other words, before you make your first $10 profit, you will need to sell 1,000 shirts. Can you sell at least 1,001 shirts? If not, you should not go ahead with the venture.

Now, try doing a break-even analysis yourself.

CALCULATING THE BREAK-EVEN POINT FOR A SEMINAR

Suppose you were running a seminar on word-processing programs to promote your computer store. You plan to charge a $50 admission. The speaker's lecture fee is $1,800. You plan to provide lunches at a cost of $10 per attendee. At what point would you break even on the seminar?

○ What is your fixed cost?
○ What is your variable cost?
○ What is your selling price?
○ How many admission tickets (units) must you sell to break even?

Did you arrive at 45 tickets? If not, check your math.

Calculating Break-Even by Sales Revenue in Dollars

This method allows you to calculate how many dollars in sales you need in order to break even.

Let *BEP* = dollars in sales required
FC = total fixed costs
1 = the number one
VC = variable cost of one item
SP = selling price of one item

The formula is:

$$BEP = \frac{FC}{1 - \dfrac{VC}{SP}}$$

or

$$BEP = \frac{\$10,000}{1 - \dfrac{\$15}{\$25}}$$

then

$$BEP = \frac{\$10,000}{1 - .6}$$

or

$$BEP = \frac{\$10,000}{.4}$$

therefore

$$BEP = \$25,000$$

In other words, you need to sell $25,000 worth of shirts to recover your advertising (fixed) cost of $10,000 plus your variable cost (the cost of the shirts). Now you have broken even; the next shirt sold will yield a profit on this particular venture.

For more complex situations, you may need to average both the sales price and the cost of goods. If you are graphically inclined, you may prefer to chart your break-even analysis on graph paper. Use points along the bottom of the graph to represent units sold and points along the side to represent dollar volume. Then plot your fixed costs with one line (FC) and your variable costs with another (VC). Your break-even point is the point where the lines intersect.

What If I Won't Break Even?

Suppose you find that you must sell an unrealistically high number of items or take in an unrealistically high amount of money to break even. Before you abandon the idea of going into business, consider these alternatives. You might:

○ Increase your selling price
○ Reduce your variable costs
○ Reduce your fixed costs

Before you increase prices, you need to be sure that the increase will not reduce demand to the point where you are worse off than before. In other words, if raising your prices by 30 percent would reduce your unit sales by 35 percent, your income would actually decrease.

Perhaps you can reduce variable costs in some way. Can you purchase goods at a lower price? Reduce commissions? Find less expensive ways to wrap or deliver goods? So long as these measures do not decrease your sales volume, they may improve your break-even situation.

Can you reduce fixed costs? Perhaps you can effectively reduce your rent by leasing space to another person or by taking over some services the landlord provided. Can you lower your advertising or insurance costs? Be careful not to lower costs in a way that jeopardizes your business in the long term.

Perhaps you are pursuing "the best quality" and "the best service" when your customers would be better served at a slightly lower level of service reflected in a lower price. After all, continuity of service is important to customers too.

HOW MANY SANDWICHES PER COUNTER STOOL?

Joe was upset when he called me in as a consultant. "Help! I've been in business almost a year and I'm losing my shirt!" Joe's snack shop was in a good location. Customers seemed to like his sandwiches. But his income wasn't covering his expenses.

The first thing I did was to calculate his break-even point. Joe's monthly fixed outlays were:

Rent	$ 800
Insurance	100
Loan payment	400
Utilities	200
Wages	800
	$ 2300

His customers' average check came to $4.00, for which his materials costs (variable costs) for lunch meat, paper plates, bread, drinking straws, ketchup, mayonnaise, and so forth came to $2.00.

How many lunches would Joe have to serve in order to break even?

$$BE = \frac{\$2,300}{\$4.00 - \$2.00}$$

$$BE = \frac{\$2,300}{\$2.00}$$

$$BE = 1,150$$

To break even on lunches alone, Joe needed to sell 1,150 sandwiches per month. Divided by 22 business days a month (Joe was only open during the week because his trade came from nearby offices), that came out to about 93 sandwiches a day. Joe's small shop had only six counter stools. Even if half his business were takeout, he would have to sell more than 45 sandwiches at the counter each day to break even. With six stools, that meant he would have to serve five customers at each stool between 12 and 1:30 or so. Even if his customers averaged only 20 minutes per lunch, he couldn't break even.

What could Joe do? Raising prices wasn't the answer; competition was too keen. Joe considered adding a breakfast menu—coffee, doughnuts, pastries. That would have little effect on his fixed costs. He added some high-ticket items to the lunch menu. He also decided to promote his takeout business and to focus on that rather than on-premises sales. He did so well that he soon removed all six stools! Break-even analysis showed the way.

Calculating Your Owner's Equity

To complete your financial planning, you need to prepare a **balance sheet.** This computation shows the properties your business owns (assets), the debts your business owes (liabilities), and the difference between them, which constitutes your **owner's equity** or **net worth.** Here is a typical balance sheet.

You should prepare projected balance sheets for at least three years of business operation during your planning phase.

CURRENT BALANCE SHEET FOR

_____
(name of your firm)

As of _____
(date)

Assets		Liabilities and Capital	
Current Assets:		**Current Liabilities:**	
Cash in bank	$____	Accounts payable	$____
Petty cash	____	Notes payable due	
Accounts receivable	____	within one year	____
Less allowance for		Payroll taxes and	
doubtful accounts	−____	withheld taxes	____
Merchandise inventories	____	Sales taxes	____
Total current assets	$____	Total current liabilities	$____
Fixed Assets:		**Long-term Liabilities:**	
Land	____	Notes payable, due	
Building	____	after one year	____
Delivery equip.	____	Total long-term liabilities	____
Furniture and			
fixtures	____	Total liabilities	____
Less allowance for			
depreciation	−____	**Capital:**	
Leasehold improvements	____	Proprietor's capital,	
Less amortization	−____	beginning of period	____
Total fixed assets	____	Net profit for the	
		period	____
TOTAL ASSETS	$____	Less proprietor's	
		drawings	−____
		Increase in capital	____
		Total capital end of period	____
		TOTAL LIABILITIES AND CAPITAL $____	

Your balance sheet shows you whether your investment in your business is increasing or decreasing in value over time.

Planning Is Not a Onetime Activity

Don't just prepare a business plan and then follow it blindly. Reexamine your plans and update them according to your experience. Where are your financial weaknesses? What can you do to improve your profits?

To start your business, you may need more money than you now have. Should you save more cash before starting? Should you borrow from a relative or friend? Do you need a bank loan? Credit from suppliers? Careful, detailed, thorough financial plans enable you to make sound decisions about your business; they also are the key to financing your new enterprise.

CHAPTER FIVE

Getting Practical Help and Obtaining Financing

KEY TERMS

ACE/SCORE program   *SBA guaranty loan*
SBA direct loan   *U.S. Small Business Administration (SBA)*

No matter what kind of business you decide on, there are some start-up activities, including paperwork, that you'll have to go through. You may be wondering where you can find practical assistance with all the details of starting and running a small business. And, unless you have considerable savings and plan to plunge them all into your business, you'll be needing loans for business equipment or property as well as credit from suppliers.

Before You Start

Of course, you'll want to name your business. Some considerations about your business name and image have to do with marketing and are discussed in Chapter 9. For now, consider whether you'll be using your own name or what the law calls a "fictitious name." If you're going to call yourself Linda Jones and Associates, the ownership of your business is clear, but its purpose is not. If you're going to call yourself Laziday Laundry Service, your purpose is clear but the ownership is not. You will have to file your name and ownership with your state and possibly also with your municipality or county. Your state's department of commerce or industry can help.

Some states, counties, or municipalities require that all businesses, regardless of name, be registered with the county clerk. Your financial institution may require a copy of this registration before approving a business loan. Again, you can inquire with the state. Your telephone directory will list municipal departments as well as state departments where you can inquire.

If your state has a sales tax, you will need to register as a collector of sales taxes. The same goes for state income or unemployment taxes and workers' compensation.

The Internal Revenue Service requires that you have a federal employment identification number in order to collect employee taxes; this number is also used in many business transactions. Contact your nearest IRS office (see the telephone book under U.S. Government) and ask for Form SS-4. Without an F.E.I.N. number, your business transactions will be associated with your own social security number, and this could cause you problems at tax time.

County, state, and federal agencies generally use the same federal I.D. number as the IRS.

Contact your state's department of labor to find out what records you must keep to comply with state wage and hour laws.

From the IRS, obtain a Small Business Tax Kit. This will provide you with current information about your tax obligations both as an employer and as a small-business proprietor.

You should also make sure that you are not violating any zoning or land use regulations by operating a business on your premises. Your local zoning board can provide copies of zoning regulations as well as zoning maps for you to study. It may be necessary to apply for a zoning permit, a nonconforming use variance, and/or a building permit. Visit or call your local building inspector. Inquire with the fire department and the health department. What are the local rules about signs, display window area, plumbing and electrical work, occupancy rates?

Other possible regulations include sanitation rules, environmental rules, and so on. It is impossible to cover them all in a book of this kind because of local variations and continually changing laws and regulations.

By now you may be feeling overwhelmed by the potential paperwork. Some of it can wait until tax time; at this point you just need to make sure that no untoward surprises are waiting for you. Concentrate on identifying your market and making sure your business is financially feasible. When you are ready to cope with paperwork, there's help to be had for the asking.

Help! Where Do I Find It?

You are not alone. Help is available for small entrepreneurs from both government and private organizations, national

THE STAGES OF A BUSINESS

Like every business, yours can be expected to go through four stages: survivability, growth, profitability, and decline. Your objective should be to achieve the first three and avoid the fourth as long as possible.

○ **Survivability.** When you are forming your business, you are spending a great deal of money just to get started. You have to buy or lease equipment, invest in furniture and fixtures, experiment with new products or services, find markets, promote your name. The money coming in may be barely enough to meet your bills.

○ **Growth.** Once your business has survived its start-up problems, it enters an era of growth. Income may exceed current expenses, but you'll need to reinvest surplus funds to hire more staff and buy more equipment. Additional customers make your business grow, but that means spending more on materials, inventory, supplies, and wages.

○ **Profitability.** When your business reaches its desired sales level, profit becomes available to you. The business brings in enough money to pay for supplies, materials, and personnel. Surplus funds need no longer go for expansion.

○ **Decline.** No sooner is it evident that a business is prospering than competitors enter the scene. They will attempt to produce a better product or service, and to produce it more cheaply. Profit margins will be lower as you struggle to compete. The less efficient competitors will be forced out of business. Those that fail to devise a better product/service/price "package" for their customers will decline. This is the time when you must emphasize marketing, develop new products and services, become more efficient.

Business enterprises are like trees in the forest. They sprout, they struggle to grow, they flourish for a season, they decline. Some seedlings perish. Some trees are felled by lightning. As trees need nourishment, sunlight, and rain, businesses need sound financing, effective marketing, and adequate sales volume.

and local. Much of this assistance is tax-supported and therefore available at no charge to you; some is available at nominal cost.

Your Banker Can Help

Commercial banks have commercial loan officers whose job is to assist businesses in obtaining financing. If your business is very small, you may want to look for a smaller bank that makes an effort to attract small-business customers. Banks want to lend money—that's how they make money. A loan officer can help you analyze your business plan and may have helpful suggestions. Banks are usually well aware of local business and economic patterns; use yours as a resource.

Your Accountant and Your Lawyer Can Help

Accountants and lawyers each have their place in helping you get started. An accountant can help formulate your business plans, estimate tax consequences, and spot weaknesses in your financial projections. Your attorney can help draw up contracts, evaluate leases and other business contracts, and advise you about insurance, legal liability, local regulations, and other potential pitfalls.

Check Out Your Library

Besides general books on small business like this one, there are many books about specific kinds of businesses. There are trade and professional journals as well as magazines for the general public such as *Money* magazine, which often runs articles about entrepreneurs. Larger libraries will have *Inc, Entrepreneur's Magazine*, and similar publications. Familiarize yourself with the many business periodicals and books in your library's reference section.

What Do Local Colleges Offer?

In one eastern Pennsylvania community, the county Chamber of Commerce offers a whole series of inexpensive small-business courses at the local community college. These courses are taught by active businesspeople and cover such areas as hiring employees, taxes, legal considerations, financial planning, and marketing. These offerings are typical of what is available nationwide.

In addition, three quarters of U.S. colleges offer some kind of business curriculum. Call your local colleges and universities for names of their business faculty. Write or call for an appointment. Business professors can give you helpful information about advertising, salesmanship, and many other aspects of business.

The SBA Can Help

In 1963, the U.S. Congress created the **U.S. Small Business Administration (SBA)** to provide various kinds of assistance to small entrepreneurs, including counseling and business loans. What constitutes a small business? Mainly, a business must be (1) independently owned, (2) locally operated, and (3) not dominant in its field. Regulations about dollar volume and number of employees vary according to the type of business. In general, a business is considered "small" if it grosses less than $3 million annually and employs fewer than 100 employees. Under this broad definition, 95 percent of U.S. businesses can be classified as small.

A valuable service provided by the SBA is its **ACE/SCORE program.** ACE stands for Active Corps of Executives; SCORE stands for Service Corps of Retired Executives. ACE/SCORE volunteers are capable, seasoned business advisers who provide free counseling to entrepreneurs.

For assistance with start-up or ongoing problems, don't hesitate to telephone the SBA. Look in the white pages of your phone book under U.S Government. Main offices of the SBA are in the state capitals; contact the main office to inquire about the nearest regional office that has an ACE/SCORE program. The counseling will be free and confidential.

Your Local Government May Help

Many larger communities have some kind of industrial or commercial development program. Such programs can offer low-interest financing, rental space in rehabilitated buildings, and other assistance to new businesses.

Obtaining Financing for Your Venture

Sooner or later, you will need to borrow money for your business.

Stategies for Successful Loan Seeking

When you are ready to approach a lending institution, these strategies can help increase your chances for success.

○ *Pick the right lending agency.* For a business loan, go to a commercial bank. For a real estate mortgage loan, try a savings and loan institution. For a large construction loan, approach a life insurance company. To finance your inventory, go to a commercial credit agency. For a second mortgage, try a finance company—but remember, the interest will be extremely high—or perhaps the owner of the property you're buying.

○ *On your first visit, pick up an application and take it home.* Don't fill it out on the spot. Get your accountant to assist you. Do a "trial run" on a photocopy, then have the final version typed.

○ *Don't go unannounced.* Be professional. Make an appointment with a loan officer in advance.

○ *Come to the meeting thoroughly prepared.* Bring the financial plans you worked so hard to make. Bring your accounting statements and/or projections: balance sheet, cash flow projections, break-even analysis, operating statements. Bring a list of your personal assets and outstanding loans; especially when you are starting, loan officers will consider your personal credit and your personal assets. Prepare an anticipated budget to show your ability to meet the loan payments. Your SBA ACE/SCORE counselor can help prepare this material.

○ *Demonstrate your character and your capacity to repay.* During the interview, mention your previous business experience and show evidence of prompt payments.

○ *Provide evidence that you know your field.* What is your training or education in the field? Have you worked in this business for someone else? Lenders need to feel that you know what you are doing, including the risks it entails.

○ *Know exactly how much you want to borrow.* Don't say, "I'll take whatever you give me." Use your financial plan to substantiate the amount you need to borrow. Allow an additional "contingency allowance" for the unexpected delay or expense. Figure in sufficient working capital to keep you in business until your accounts receivable turn into cash. Asking for a well-substantiated, specific sum shows you to be precise and accurate in your business dealings.

○ *Don't beg.* Lenders are in business to lend. You will be paying them interest. Neither of you is doing the other a favor. You are there to offer yourself as a customer and to listen to their offer—the amount they're willing to lend and the terms under which they'll lend it.

○ *Think things over before signing.* Think the offer over. Can you meet the repayment terms? What security must you put up? Should you shop around? A difference of only .5 percent in the interest rate can come to a large sum over the duration of the loan.

Once you have the loan, put that borrowed money to work. Increase your working capital by improving your credit policies. Be selective in offering credit, and be diligent in pursuing delinquent accounts. At the same time, pay your own bills as late as you can without jeopardizing your credit. The sooner you collect what's owed you and the later you pay what you owe, the more cash you have to work with.

The SBA Loan Program

The U.S. Small Business Administration has a loan assistance program designed for entrepreneurs who cannot obtain financing directly through private lenders. Since laws and regulations change, you should contact your state or local SBA office or consult your ACE/SCORE counselor to obtain current information. Remember that you may be asked to document that you have tried conventional sources and been turned down.

The following information is taken from the government publication *Business Loans from the SBA*, issued by the Office of Public Communications, June 1987 (publication OPC-6):

The SBA offers two basic types of loans, direct and guaranty, to businesses that otherwise meet the eligibility requirements below. **Direct loans** are made with SBA funds. They are available only to certain classifications of borrowers, such as businesses in areas of high unemployment, or businesses owned by handicapped persons, disabled veterans, or veterans of the Vietnam War. These eligibility requirements change from time to time, but as of the fiscal year 1987, direct loans were available only for the following (and only if these persons had been turned down for a guaranty loan):

MURPHY'S LAW AND YOUR BUSINESS

You've heard of Murphy's Law: "If anything can go wrong, it will." A corollary of that law is, "Everything takes longer than planned." Don't go into business thinking you can escape Murphy.

The zoning change takes three hearings instead of one. Your newly hired employee doesn't show up. The factory sends the wrong machine. Your shipment gets held up in a blizzard. A hurricane hits town on Grand Opening Day.

Expect delays. Plan for them.

When you can't open your new business, sales revenues will be delayed. If you miss a critical season or holiday, revenues may be reduced altogether.

The worst commodity you can run out of is money. When you make your financial plans, be sure there's a Plan B that you can plug in when Murphy strikes Plan A.

○ Veterans from the Vietnam era (1964–75) who served on active duty for more than 180 days, any part of which fell between 5 August 1964 and 7 May 1975.
○ Disabled veterans from any era with a service-connected disability of 30 percent or more.
○ Any veteran with a disability discharge.
○ Handicapped individuals unable to obtain a regular bank loan or an SBA guaranty loan.

Proof of refusal of a regular or guaranty loan may be a written statement from the lender containing the date, the amount requested, the terms discussed, and the reason for declining the loan.

Guaranty loans are not made with government funds; instead, the SBA guarantees repayment to the lenders, usually banks, of up to 90 percent of the principal. You, the borrower, fill out the application and submit it to the lender. The lender reviews the application initially, then forwards it to the SBA. If the SBA approves the loan, they disburse the funds to you.

To be eligible for an SBA loan, you must meet certain criteria. Your business:

○ Must be operated for profit
○ Must meet certain size criteria
○ Must not be involved in the creation or distribution of ideas or opinions (it cannot be a newspaper, magazine, or school, for example)
○ Must not be involved in speculation or investment in rental real estate

Criteria for size are based on the average number of employees for the preceding twelve-month period or on sales volume averaged over a three-year period. The maximum allowable limit depends on the type of business:

○ Manufacturing: 500 to 1,500 employees, depending on the type of product

○ Wholesaling: 100 employees

○ Service: annual receipts of no more than $3.5 to $14.5 million, depending on the industry

○ Retailing: annual receipts of no more than $3.5 to $13.5, depending on the industry

○ Construction: annual receipts of no more than $9.5 to $17 million, depending on the industry

○ Special trade construction: annual receipts of no more than $7 million

○ Agriculture: annual receipts of no more than $550,000 to $3.5 million, depending on the industry

Collateral requirements. The SBA also requires that sufficient collateral be pledged to adequately secure the loan. All principal owners and the chief executive of the business must provide personal guarantees. If the business assets are not sufficient to secure the loan, liens may be placed on personal assets.

Credit requirements. The loan applicant must be of good character, must demonstrate sufficient management expertise, and must reveal a commitment to successful operation. The applicant must have enough capital so that, with the SBA loan, the business can operate on a sound financial basis. This includes sufficient funds to cover start-up expenses during the initial phase when losses are most likely to occur. Generally, the SBA requires that from one third to one half the total assets needed to launch a new business be invested by the owner.

Not everyone who asks for an SBA loan receives one. These loans may not be obtained, for example, to pay current bills or to pay taxes.

What the SBA and the Lender Will Want to Know

Start by obtaining an appointment with an SBA ACE/SCORE counselor. He or she will assist you with your loan application. You will need the following information. When you have compiled it and it is in the best possible shape, take it to your commercial bank and apply for a loan directly. If you are turned down, ask the bank to contact the SBA for discussion of your application. Usually the SBA will deal directly with the bank.

If your application for a guaranty loan is turned down, obtain a written proof of refusal. Then, if you qualify for a direct loan, take your refusal letter to the SBA office together with your supporting information. They will help you proceed from there.

For a Loan to Start a New Business

You will need:

- A detailed description of the proposed business
- A description of your trade or management experience
- An estimate of how much you (and any partners or members of your corporation) can invest and how much you need to borrow
- A financial statement (see Chapter 4)
- A detailed earnings projection for your first year (see Chapter 4)
- A list of all collateral you are offering as security and its current market value

To Purchase an Existing Business

- A detailed description of the business to be purchased, including the reason it is being sold
- A description of your trade and management experience
- An estimate of how much you and others will invest in the business
- How much you need to borrow and how you will allocate the funds
- A current personal balance sheet for each of the principals, listing all assets and liabilities
- Detailed projections of first-year earnings, together with an explanation of how you expect to achieve that level of revenue
- A list of all collateral and the current market value of each item
- The following material from the present owner:

1. Current balance sheet and operating statement
2. The past three years' federal income tax returns, signed and dated by the seller
3. The proposed bill of sale, including the terms of sale and the asking price with a schedule of inventory, machinery and equipment, furniture and fixtures

To Obtain a Loan for an Established Business

You will need:

- Current financial statement (balance sheet) listing business assets and liabilities (exclude personal items)
- Operating (profit and loss) statement showing revenues and expenses for the preceding year and for the current year to date
- Current personal financial statement for yourself, for each partner, and for each stockholder owning more than 20 percent of the business
- List of collateral with current market value
- The amount of the loan requested and the exact purposes for which it will be used

You can expand on or substantiate this information with your break-even analysis and other detailed portions of your financial plan; also include your business plan. Refer to Chapters 3 and 4.

PITFALLS THAT LEAD TO LOAN REFUSALS

○ Lack of careful preparation
○ Insufficient information
○ Poor organization
○ Vagueness leading to poor credibility
○ Lack of clarity; illegibility
○ Failure to plan ahead
○ Requesting a loan for personal salary
○ Requesting a loan to pay current bills or taxes
○ And, of course, a bad credit history

The material pertaining to loan applications was prepared with the generous assistance of Mr. Theodore Luszcz, Director, Newark, New Jersey, Office, U.S. Small Business Administration.

PART TWO

MANAGING AND MARKETING YOUR BUSINESS

CHAPTER SIX

The Computer and Your Business

KEY TERMS

database programs	mail-merging program	software
disk operating system	microcomputer (PC)	spreadsheet program
floppy disk	microprocessor	storage drive
hard disk	RAM	system unit (CPU)
hardware	ROM	word processing

As recently as the early 1980s, few small businesses were likely to have computers—especially at start-up time. Today, the situation has changed. Prices have come down; a system that would have filled up a whole room and cost millions when computers were first developed will fit into a briefcase for portable use and costs a few thousand dollars or less. Today's computers are versatile, compact, and inexpensive—especially when you consider what a computer can do.

Because computer technology changes even from month to month, it's not practical to try to give you detailed advice. Instead, this chapter focuses on some of the most basic computer terms and computer functions to help you when you investigate on your own.

What a Computer Can Do for Your Business

First, computers can do what they are best known for: "number crunching." You are doubtless aware that a computer can do your bookkeeping. But you may not realize how wide a range of activities the computer can help with. For example, it can:

○ Total and send out bills

○ Pay invoices—including writing the checks

○ Maintain and update inventories

○ Create and maintain categorized mailing lists: customers who bought widgets, customers who have bought something last month—or nothing for twelve months, potential customers, customers who spend more or less than specified amount, customers who live in the area of a proposed branch

○ Create and update financial projections and present them in graphic form (bar graphs, pie charts, etc.)

○ Inform you which products and services are selling well and which are not—and to whom

○ Maintain customer records and "reminder" lists

○ Transmit orders or bids via telephone lines

○ Receive information from centralized data bases by telephone line

○ Create and print illustrated customer newsletters

It's *not* true, no matter what the salesperson says, that computers can do all this "at the push of a button." Entering and using computerized data takes practice, but today's equipment and programs are designed to be user-friendly. Community colleges and computer sales organizations offer seminars and courses to help you get the most out of your equipment.

Very early in your business life—perhaps even before the business is operating—you should investigate what a computer could do for you. The computer can make your financial planning easier and faster, and for that very reason you will be more thorough and precise in your planning. For example, you can do a break-even analysis, then change one factor—say, the cost of a crucial material—and have the results on the screen in seconds. You can do the same thing with operating projections and balance sheets: What difference would it make if you leased equipment instead of buying and depreciating it? You can also project the effect that different decisions would have on your taxes.

In considering a computer for your business, you will need to know some common terms that are used to describe what a computer system will do and how it operates. It's common to think first in terms of equipment ("hardware"), but in fact you should not choose equipment until you've given some thought to what you will be doing with it—now and in the future. Hardware is the brain and brawn of a computer system; software is the intelligence or mind. Not all software can be "run" (used) on all hardware.

Software: The Intelligence of the System

Software programs are the intellect of any computer system. Programs "decide" what to do and tell the equipment how to do it. Programs consist of complex chains of logic "written" in specialized "languages" that basically consist of a series of "ons" and "offs." *You do not need to know how to program in order to use a computer in your business.* Many "introduction to the computer" courses still attempt to teach programming, but in fact programs for every conceivable use (called "applications" in computer jargon) can be purchased off the shelf. If modifications are needed for your particular business, consultants are available to make them. Learn programming only if you think you have an aptitude for it or would enjoy it. (You may surprise yourself.)

Operating Software

In order to work, a computer requires **operating system software.** These programs control the keyboard, the monitor (screen), and many internal operations. In addition, operational software for a personal computer includes the **operating system** by which the computer "reads," "writes," and stores information. The importance of your operating system is that it determines which programs will work with your system. *A program written for one type of operating system may not be operable on a different system.* In that sense, the software you want to use determines what hardware you buy.

Until quite recently, the most popular operating system for microcomputers (PCs) was MS-DOS and its IBM version, PC-DOS. A new, faster operating system called OS/2 has now been introduced and may supplant MS-DOS eventually. As of this writing, the vast majority of small-business software was designed for MS-DOS, and consequently the vast majority

of computers used by small businesses were IBM or IBM-compatible. ("Compatible" means that software developed for the IBM can be run on the compatible computer.) It is expected that OS/2 systems will be able to run the more popular MS/DOS software and use data generated with the older system.

The major competing, non-IBM system is that used by Apple. Apple computers are heavily used in certain businesses where their graphics and "desktop publishing" abilities are especially useful.

Applications Programs

You can buy applications programs for accounting, word processing, payroll processing—virtually any business function.

Spreadsheet programs are especially useful in accounting because they enable you to view a broad range of data and then quickly calculate the effect of any change. At present the most popular spreadsheet program is Lotus 1-2-3. These programs are complicated and somewhat difficult to learn. **Database programs,** as the name suggests, store and categorize data—including inventory, for example. They enable you to classify information by fields, so that you can quickly call up such information as the names of customers who purchased particular products. The best-known database program is currently dBase III.

Word processing programs, as the name suggests, can get out your letters and reports. Together with a **mail-merging** feature they can be used to address mailing lists. Today's word processing programs often contain spelling checkers (internal, or "resident" dictionaries) and some will even call your attention to common grammatical errors. **Integrated software programs** contain a combination of applications such as database, accounting, and word processing.

Features to Look for in Software

Before you buy any software, look carefully at its "documentation," as instruction manuals are called in the trade. Is it clear? Is the index comprehensive? *Can you understand it?* Does it include an interactive tutorial so that you can learn by doing?

Prices vary. Developing new software is very time-consuming and expensive; the small plastic disk you are holding in your hand can represent thousands of hours of programming research. If the resulting software has many potential users (word processing, for example), the price may be relatively low; if there are few potential users, the price must be higher. The com-

---

QUESTIONS TO ASK YOUR SOFTWARE SALESPERSON

○ Will this run on my system?

○ How much RAM (random access memory) does it require? (This may be stated on the carton or in the literature.)

○ Do you have a sample I can try out here?

○ May I see the manual?

○ Is an interactive tutorial available?

○ Does the price include on-site training of myself and/or my staff?

○ Does the software company have a hotline? Is it toll-free?

○ Are updates available to owners at a reduced price?

○ Can you give me names of customers with businesses like mine who use this software?

○ For customer programs: Will you certify in writing that the program will perform the specified tasks?

○ Is the program compatible with other standard software; can data be swapped from one to the other?

○ For word processing: Is this a WYSIWYG format (`what you see [on the screen] is what you get")?

plexity of the program makes a difference, too. Be wary of bargains. One "bargain" accounting program requires that you first print out its 100-page manual; then you must print out the results of your calculations before you can evaluate them—they are not displayed on the screen.

You should also be aware of update availability. Software is continually being improved. Many companies make updates available at low cost to registered purchasers. Other considerations include speed (some software is comparatively fast, other software slow). Performance is a major consideration, especially if you are having software designed for your particular business. Get written confirmation from the vendor that the program will do what it is supposed to do. Talk with other users if at all possible.

You will also have to consider the capacity of your equipment. Remember that the software program itself takes up some of the RAM (see page 69)—often 40k or more. The amount of data you can actually work with is limited by what the software takes up. Also consider the amount of data your system can store. See the discussion of hardware.

"Bundled software" is a term referring to software programs offered with a computer as a sales inducement. Bundled software can save you money *if it is compatible with other programs you will be using*. A "bundle" that includes recognized, widely used programs is valuable. One that includes programs that will run only on a particular brand of computer is of dubious value. Even if you don't anticipate using other programs, it will limit your ability to "import" data obtained from another system—for example, a mailing list.

Computer magazines regularly review software programs. Often they provide charts showing comparative features.

Hardware: The Brains and Brawn of the System

The discussion of computer hardware in this chapter is limited to currently available **microcomputers** (PCs—formerly called personal computers). Today's sophisticated systems have sufficient capacity for most small businesses, especially those just starting out.

If you look at a PC, its obvious components are its **system unit** (also referred to as the central processing unit, or CPU); the keyboard, which may or may not be directly attached to the CPU; and the **monitor,** or CRT. One or more **storage drives**, which "read" and "write" data, are generally contained in the same case as the CPU. **Peripherals** are auxiliary equipment—that is, the computer can operate without them. The principal peripheral you will need is a printer of some kind; you may also want a modem, which permits the computer to receive and transmit data over telephone lines.

The System Unit

The heart of the system unit is its **microprocessor.** It manipulates all data in terms of the on/off condition of its registers. The smallest parcel of information is a *bit;* eight bits make a binary number (that is, a number consisting entirely of 0's and 1's) and are referred to as a *byte*. For example, when you strike the letter "e" or the number 9 on the keyboard, it is translated into a series of 0's and 1's in order for the microprocessor to handle it.

The capacity of computers is measured in terms of bytes, usually expressed in terms of kilobytes or megabytes. One kilobyte (1k) equals 1,024 bytes; one megabyte (1Mb) equals 1,048,576 bytes. A computer with 256k capacity, once considered ample but now considered marginal, can manipulate more than a quarter-million bytes (numbers or letters). (You can store any amount of information on disks or tape, but the computer can handle only a specified amount at one time.)

In addition to the microprocessor, the CPU contains internal electronic linkages that allow communication among the keyboard, the storage drives, the monitor, and so on. The microprocessor can only "concentrate" on a few items at a time, so it must continually refer to its **RAM,** or random access memory. Capacity specifications (256k, etc.) refer to the RAM. The computer also has an internal, permanent memory—the **ROM,** or read-only memory—to store operating information. The user can address (enter or delete data) the RAM but not the ROM.

So long as it is in the RAM, information is not permanent. Turning off the system—or even a brief power interruption—causes the data to be lost, as many first-time computer users have found to their dismay. Also, the capacity of the RAM is limited. To be retained permanently, data must be stored on a magnetic medium such as magnetic tape or magnetic disks.

VALERIE'S SPREADSHEET VANISHED IN AN EYEBLINK

"I've got to get these projections done," thought Valerie. "I'm meeting with the bank tomorrow." It was already 1 A.M., and Valerie felt as though her eyes were dancing with green-and-black specks. The spreadsheet program was complicated and a bit unfamiliar, and Valerie concentrated on adjusting her break-even to every circumstance the banker was likely to raise. She knew she should save her data to the disk—the saleswoman had certainly stressed the importance of doing so. "In a minute," she kept thinking, "just as soon as I—"

WHAM! Valerie jumped. A car had hit a light pole just outside her window. The lights blinked out, then came on again. Valerie watched in horror as her spreadsheet projection shrank to a tiny green dot, then vanished from the screen. The computer came back on—but Valerie's projection had vanished.

The Storage Drives

Material in the RAM vanishes the instant you turn the computer off. Programs are stored on magnetic media and fed into the RAM as needed, and the information you are entering and working with must be periodically "saved." (This does not occur automatically; it requires an instruction from the user.) The most common storage media for PCs are removable **floppy disks,** permanent **hard disks,** and magnetic tapes for backup storage. The read/write head of the disk drive moves quickly from one part of the disk to another to transmit data to the RAM or to store it. You use your operating system to "format" blank diskettes with invisible "tracks" that enable the read/write head to locate information. (This computer technology is used in compact-disk recording of music.)

Floppy disks come in several sizes and capacities. The type of disk drive you have determines the type of disk you must use, and consequently the amount of data you can store on a single disk. The size currently in most common use is the 5-inch floppy; 3.5-inch disks are becoming more popular. Disk storage capacities range from 360k to 1.44Mb.

Hard disks are permanently fixed, unlike floppy disks, which can be removed and inserted by the user. Currently available hard disk capacity ranges from 10Mb to 200Mb. This means that large volumes of information can be accessed at once. For example, a 10Mb hard disk can store up to 6,000 double-spaced pages of text. Programs can be stored on the hard disk also. In a hard disk system, floppy disks are used to make separate backup files.

Hard disk systems are much faster than those employing floppy disks. They are also more expensive, but their speed and their potential for expansion of the system are major advantages.

Monitors

Monitors resemble TV screens. Like TV screens, they display information in the form of dots (called pixels). The more dots, the clearer the picture. The steadiness of the picture (lack of flicker) is also important. Many computer stores are now displaying color monitors; consider carefully before purchasing one. In general, color monitors are not as clear as monochrome monitors (which are usually green or amber and black). Do you really need color? To display color, the system must be equipped with a "color card." To display information in the form of graphics, you will need a "graphics card." Both these features are additional-cost options.

Printers

You will want to be able to print out your data and, probably, to use your computer for word processing. **Dot matrix printers** form characters by impressing a pattern of dots. The resolution (clarity) of the result depends on the number of pins in the print head and the number of times each character is struck. The condition of the ribbon also affects the printed image.

Dot matrix printers can print very fast. When they do, however, the dots are far apart and the image tends to be faint. The letters may not look like print or typewriting. Many of today's dot matrix printers overcome this deficiency by having speed adjustments—fast for rough copies and numerical data, slow for "letter quality."

These printers can reproduce graphic images. With specialized software, they can print sideways—an advantage in producing large spreadsheets.

Wheel printers are like computerized typewriters. They imprint by means of the familiar "golf ball," a daisy wheel, or a thimble. The result looks like first-quality typing. If the appearance of your letters is extremely important—for example, if your business caters to a luxury trade—you may need a wheel printer. These printers are slow, noisy, and expensive, and they are not suited to printing graphical displays.

Laser printers produce an image in a manner similar to photocopying machines. They are fast, versatile, and quiet. At present, laser printers are far more expensive than dot matrix printers—$2,000 or more compared to $400 or less. In time the price may well come down. If you are thinking of doing large mailings or customer newsletters at your location (there are businesses that will do this for you), you may find a laser printer worth the investment.

You may start with an inexpensive printer and trade up later. Some printers use a tractor feed and require the type of paper that comes in perforated sheets with holed strips at the edge. Others will print on individual sheets, and some can use either. You can now purchase stationery, labels, even checks in tractor-feed form.

What to Look for in Hardware

Of course, you want reliability. Monitors and CPU have no moving parts; any problems are likely to crop up during the warranty period. Storage drives are more fragile; printers are the most likely to be troublesome, because of their many rapidly moving parts. Check the warranties and ask for data on the "mean time between failures" (MTBF) for comparison purposes. An MTBF rating of 15,000 hours or better is considered good. Don't be surprised if the saleperson has to dig for this information.

Speed may be a consideration. Computers are inherently so much faster than pencil calculating that you may be surprised at how impatient you become waiting 15 seconds for what would formerly have taken you an hour to do. Speed is determined by the microprocessor and also by the "average access time" of the disk drive. Hard disk systems are faster than floppies, with access times ranging from 35 to 85 milliseconds (ms). The lower the number, the faster the time. Tape drives are used mainly for long-term data storage today because accessing data is so slow.

Two major considerations are compatibility and expandibility. You want to be able to expand your system as needed *without reentering all your data*. If you have to switch to an incompatible system in order to expand, you are very likely to have to reenter all your existing records in order to use them—a massive, expensive, time-consuming chore. In many ways, compatibility and expandibility go together. You may want to add additional computers or entry terminals that "talk" to one another. Can this be done? How many "ports" for adding peripherals does the computer have?

All these terms may seem unfamiliar and hard to learn. If you possibly can, subscribe to a magazine for PC users for a few months or a year before you buy. The reviews of equipment, the advertisements, the "help" columns, and the letters from users will help familiarize you with terms and potential problems.

SOME QUESTIONS TO ASK THE HARDWARE SALESPERSON

○ How much RAM is available?

○ How fast is the microprocessor?

○ Is the operating system included in the price? What system is it?

○ Is the system IBM-compatible? DOS-compatible?

○ What is the guarantee? Does it include both parts and labor?

○ Can I try the system at my place of business?

○ Do you do repairs on premises or send them out?

○ Do you offer "loaners" in case of breakdowns?

○ Can the RAM be expanded later?

○ Can I add more units? Will they "talk" to each other?

○ Do set-up and on-site instruction come as part of the package?

○ Do you offer seminars for users?

○ Can you give me the names of customers with businesses like mine?

CHAPTER SEVEN

Managing Your Business

Effective management is the key to business success. **Management** has been defined as the art and science of getting things done through other people, but it also includes effective use of your own time. As your small business grows larger, you will find yourself delegating tasks and responsibilities to others. Management is taking charge in five crucial areas: planning, organizing, staffing, leading and motivating, and exerting control.

Being good at what you do does not make you an effective manager. You can be an excellent cook, yet fail in operating a restaurant; an excellent computer programmer, yet fail in running a computer store. To operate a successful business you need strong management skills.

NINE SMALL-BUSINESS MANAGEMENT PITFALLS

Dun & Bradstreet, the well-known business rating firm, has compiled a list of nine major pitfalls identified by owners of small businesses in a nationwide survey.

- **Lack of experience.** What is needed is not experience alone, but *balanced* experience: knowing what stock to buy, how to attract customers, how to handle money.
- **Lack of money.** Lack of adequate start-up capital was identified as the second-worst pitfall. Before you start a business, use the techniques in Chapters 3 and 4 to calculate your start-up costs, determine how much money you must generate in sales to cover these expenses and provide a profit, and how you will finance the profit gap in your early days of operation.
- **Choosing the wrong location.** Location affects both your rent—a fixed expense—and the volume of business you can do. Use the guidelines in Chapter 3 to select a location appropriate to your line of business and within your means.
- **Mismanagement of inventory.** Start-up funds are limited, too much inventory is a mistake, but too little stock or too limited a range of profits can hurt you too.
- **Too large an investment in capital equipment.** The money you put into equipment, fixtures, and real property is likely to be borrowed money. If not, it comes out of your working capital—the money you need to keep going. Equipment payments can paralyze your business by leaving you with insufficient cash to operate or to adjust to unexpected situations.
- **Poor credit-granting practices.** Before you allow customers to buy on credit, make sure your cash flow will not be adversely affected—and make sure you have the skills and the tenacity to collect what is owed you.
- **Drawing too much out for yourself.** Before you embark on a business, check your personal budget. How long can you hold out without a salary? Drawing money out too soon or during a slow period can jeopardize your whole investment.
- **Unplanned expansion.** Should you open a branch? Hire more help? Enlarge your premises? Growth by addition or expansion should be carefully planned. Gaining too many customers too fast can be as harmful as not having enough, since you will not be able to satisfy their needs.
- **Having the wrong attitude.** If you start your own business, you must expect long hours, hard work, and little pay in the beginning. If you resent these conditions, your resentment will be reflected in your dealings with customers, employees, and suppliers. The right attitude can make up for other deficiencies; the wrong attitude can destroy a business that appears to have everything going for it.

Planning

Essentially, planning is thinking ahead. **Planning** is the mental activity of visualizing—right now—where you want your business to be in a month, a year, or a decade. When you plan, you bring events about and make use of circumstances instead of being their prisoner. A good plan will serve your business well even if you execute it poorly, but to fail to plan is to plan to fail.

Chapters 3 and 4 described many of the activities involved in planning. Suppose you want to open a health food store, a cleaning business, or an electronics repair service. You pick up a pencil and start making lists. You describe your business, the equipment you need, the stock you must buy, the money you must spend, when your business will open, who will staff it, and what each person will do.

When you plan, you move from the general to the specific, from the broad view to a narrow focus. Suppose you need beauty-shop equipment. That is the broad view. How many hair dryers will you need? How many sinks? Counters? Scissors? Combs? Who sells these items? How much do they cost? How will you have them installed? Are there seminars to teach you how to use them? Can you save money by buying used equipment? By leasing? By sharing? That is the specific view.

Long-Range Planning

Long-range planning should precede short-range planning, because your short-term plans should arise from your plans for the future. Where do you want your business to be five years from now? Ten years? Perhaps you envision your business reaching a certain size, then stabilizing. That, too, requires a plan.

It's a mistake to believe that you can maintain your business at a given level without planning and without changes. Buildings and equipment fall into disrepair. Customer tastes change. New developments arise. If your business sells groceries, how would you keep up with customers' demand for prepared foods? Fresh-ground coffee? More fish and poultry? Less meat? And so on.

Often day-to-day involvement with a business consumes an owner/manager's time and energy. You may view long-range planning as a luxury you'll get around to "when I have time." That can be a fatal mistake. Planning is something you have to do before your business even starts, and it's something you must keep doing as long as you stay in business.

Smart managers plan to plan. They write "June 1 and 2—Planning Days" on their calendars. They put daily work aside until they have completed the essential plans that guide them into a better business future.

The business and financial planning described in Chapters 3 and 4 is long-range planning. Your marketing plans (Chapter 9) should also be long-range as well as specific. At the conclusion of this book you'll find worksheets to help you in long-range planning for three different types of businesses.

Short-Range Planning

Your short-range plans should flow out of your long-range plans. Once you have written down your five-year objectives, you can set intermediate goals for achieving the final results. What equipment will you buy now? Next year? The year after? If you plan to have five operators and 500 customers for your beauty shop in five years, when will you hire the first operator? How will you add customers? What promotions will you carry out? What services will you start with and which will you add—and when?

Divide your goals out into six-month steps, then into monthly steps. Check them off at the appropriate times. Are you ahead or behind? Do you need to modify your goals in any way?

Take a pocket calendar and fill in your goals for each month, then the steps you will take each week to achieve them. Use the space for each Monday to list tasks for that week, then number them in order of priority.

A wall chart may also be helpful. Draw in the starting and completion dates for each item. If you have a retail clothing store, when will you start your Easter promotion? Back to School? Christmas? When must you order the stock so that it will be on display at the proper time? Do you need display materials—posters, mannequins, bunnies for Easter, tinsel for Christmas—or special printing work?

Are you enlarging your parking lot? When will this work least interfere with customer traffic? When should it be completed to allow for holiday shopping? For each of these items, back up a few days, weeks, or months and fill in such steps as ordering stock, designing and ordering advertising materials, getting bids for equipment, and so on. Have you allowed for factors such as weather? Did you allow for Murphy's Law?

GEORGE'S MINI-MALL LAID AN EGG

George planned his mini-mall as a "theme strip" aimed at small children and their parents: a clothing store, shoe store, several toy shops, school supplies, snack bar. He planned for a supervised playroom and other features to attract weary parents with one-stop shopping away from the bustle of the major mall. Originally, George intended to open at Halloween—in plenty of time for the Christmas crowds. Construction delays piled up. George knew that 50 percent of his anticipated sales would be in the Christmas season. But Easter was coming early, and he hoped to make up for lost time then. George failed to reckon with the local winter weather. The indoor contractors finished on time, but when Easter season came, the parking-lot-to-be was a mudhole cluttered with foundering bulldozers. Customers couldn't see the stores, much less shop in them. Bills piled up and interest compounded. George recovered, but it took an additional Christmas season to do it. Because of George's poor planning, his mini-mall laid an egg that gave him financial indigestion.

Organization

The second management activity, **organization,** essentially consists of grouping tasks with people. Planning indicates the results to be achieved; organizing matches tasks to be performed with the people, facilities, tools, supplies required to perform them. Neither employees nor jobs organize themselves; you, as manager, are responsible for organizing them.

Organizing your business is discussed more specifically in Chapter 8, but first let's address some general principles.

You can organize people and tasks in a number of ways:

○ By time (day, evening, and night shifts)
○ By function (the selling function, the accounting function)
○ By product or service (cameras, hardware, menswear; shampooing, haircutting, coloring)
○ By type of customer (women, men, children)
○ By department (wrapping department, service department, credit department)

Departmentation, as it is called, separates tasks into appropriate groups. This critical management task avoids conflict in the use of space, equipment, personnel, and time and thereby eases operations.

There is no single right way to create departments. The correct way is the way that operates smoothly for your particular business. Many businesses use more than one organizing principle—for example, a retail store may organize its selling space by product or customer and its office activities by function (purchasing, warehousing, shipping, maintenance).

At the beginning of your business, you may be all the departments in one; as soon as you add even a single employee, some kind of departmentalization will be necessary. Organizing the workload by departments will also help you spot problem areas and plan expansion activities.

A diagram that shows the relationships of people, tasks, and management responsibility is called an organizational chart. These charts and their uses are more fully discussed in Chapter 8.

Staffing

Once you have determined what tasks need to be performed, you must hire employees to perform them. **Staffing** consists of recruiting, interviewing, testing, screening, employing, training, and maintaining your work force. If your business sells and ships goods, you will need salespeople and shipping personnel. If you manufacture a product, you will need production workers as well as salespeople, shipping personnel, and office workers.

The recruiting function provides you with applicants, and the more successful you are in recruiting, the wider your choice and the better your chance of hiring effective workers.

Perhaps the most obvious form of recruiting is to place a Help Wanted advertisement in the local newspaper. If your work is very specialized or if the position you want to fill requires a high level of education or expertise, you may choose to advertise in trade magazines or professional journals. On the other hand, if the job is a general one, or if you expect to do most of the training yourself, on the job, you may want to recruit through a regional newspaper or even radio.

Other ways to recruit your staff include:

○ Contacting high school guidance departments

○ Notifying your community college or vocational school of openings

○ Registering with college placement centers

○ Letting current employees know about the opening; some firms even offer a bonus to employees who bring in satisfactory recruits

○ Posting notices on internal bulletin boards and in the community

○ Using employment agencies or temporary help agencies

Once you have applications, you will need to review them to select candidates for interviewing. Does the individual have special training or proof of skill? Does his or her employment record indicate reliability, or has there been shifting from job to job or unexplained periods of unemployment? Have previous jobs shown an upward progression in responsibility and pay?

Look beyond the surface. A completed application form or a résumé will tell you whether the prospective employee is neat, whether he or she can follow directions, and how much care the person takes with details. Remember, though, that a résumé

service may have prepared the information. For this reason, some employers prefer to have candidates fill out their application forms on the spot.

You can purchase standard application forms from stationery stores. If you make up your own, remember that questions pertaining to race, sex, religion, or age are against equal opportunity laws.

Leading and Motivating

Leadership is the ability to induce others to follow. This can be done through fear or by constant pushing, but the best business leaders are those who motivate people through respect and the belief that they can achieve their own personal goals through the company where they work. Effective managers learn their employees' goals and offer their employees assistance in reaching those goals.

There are many kinds and styles of leadership: dictatorship, democratic leadership, leadership by example, and low-key leadership. There is no single best style of leadership because leaders must adapt their styles to the circumstances. Leading and motivating unskilled workers to do dangerous tasks may require strict rules, high discipline, and strong authority. Leading creative people into artistic or inventive endeavors may require freedom combined with encouragement and openness.

Select a style of leadership that feels comfortable for you and appropriate for the people you want to lead.

Exerting Control

Once you have made your plans, you cannot assume that they will implement themselves. Without control, plans go astray; they take unintended directions. Your business is like a car, and you are its driver; even when it has been started up and steered in the right direction, continual small corrections must be made to keep the car on course and to avoid unanticipated obstacles and hazards.

Control has three main aspects:

○ Setting standards of performance
○ Measuring actual performance against the standards
○ Taking corrective action

Standards of performance involve not only productivity but also quality. Suppose you have determined that for you to make a profit in your floral shop, designers must complete an average of four arrangements per hour. You check their output by tallying their sales slips for the day. Now you find that over several days, one designer, Rob, is doing only three arrangements per hour worked.

The next step is to find out why. Maybe Rob is just slow. But maybe there is some other reason for his lower output. Are the largest and most intricate arrangements routinely assigned to him? If so, a standard of four per hour is simply too high. You look over the sales slips again and find that Rob's gross sales per arrangement are higher than those of the other designers. He is bringing in more money with three arrangements than the others are with four or five. In that case you might decide to leave well enough alone. Or you might

work out a productivity standard based on sales rather than units.

Or perhaps Ron is slower than the others because he takes longer to find out what customers want. He is in high demand for that reason, and you've noticed that his customers recommend your shop to their friends. In that case you might decide to leave things as they are, since Rob's value to your shop lies in customer perceptions rather than speed.

On the other hand, perhaps this arranger has farther to go to get to the coldroom where the flowers are kept. Perhaps he is nearest the phone or the cash register and is constantly being interrupted. You take corrective action as the facts warrant—but not before making sure that you know all the relevant facts. Maybe you can reorient the designers' work tables to clear a shorter path to the refrigerator. Perhaps phone or cash register duties could be rotated among the designers. It might even pay to hire a clerk to handle the phones.

Still, it is possible that Rob is simply too slow for your shop. And what about the quality of his work? You might try calling customers who received his arrangements to find out whether they were satisfied. Slow work and poor quality are an unfavorable combination; corrective action would then consist of improving Rob's performance or, if that proves impossible, firing him.

Many techniques and tools are available for exerting control. You can start with wall charts, schedules, specifications, and standard quantities or sizes. You can count, weigh, or gauge the results of work done by machines or by people. For large or repetitive operations, you might investigate statistical quality control methods.

For many small businesses, however, the owner/manager's eyes and ears, combined with financial analyses such as the break-even technique, are sufficient so long as you use them.

Once you know what is wrong or what can be improved, you can adjust machines, encourage and retrain employees, hire additional help, or whatever appears appropriate. This entails further planning as well as astute leadership.

Sometimes, especially when your business is first outgrowing your individual efforts, you'll be tempted to jump in and do the work yourself. After all, don't you know best how to do it? Probably you do. It's also true that employees can be inspired by knowing that "the boss isn't afraid to get his hands dirty." Ultimately, though, your business cannot grow and prosper until you accept the responsibility of managing: planning, organizing, staffing, leading, and controlling.

TOOLS FOR SMALL-BUSINESS MANAGEMENT

○ A **written long-range plan** that incorporates your business plan (Chapter 3), your financial plans (Chapter 4), and your marketing plan (Chapter 9), with each plan broken down into major objectives and interim goals plus the steps (strategies) for attaining them.

○ A **calendar** targeting the goals of your plans and a timetable of the strategies for achieving them. A strategy can be as simple as a phone call or as complex as a major promotional campaign. Don't forget to set aside time to plan.

○ **Employee applications;** they are vital to hiring, but don't just file them away once you've hired someone—use the information to target your employees' skills and interests.

○ **Job descriptions** that clearly outline duties and responsibilities (see Chapter 8).

○ A **written company policy** that encodes your thinking about customer service, quality standards, productivity.

○ An **organizational chart** to clarify lines of authority (see Chapter 8).

○ A **budget** of income and expense, broken down by months, with comparisons to actual outcomes.

CHAPTER EIGHT

Organizing Your Small Business

KEY TERMS

delegation
departmentation
job description

line and staff
nepotism
organizational chart
parity principle

specialization principle
unity of command
withholding taxes

When you first start your business, you may be able to run it without assistance. Sometimes the whole family pitches in on an informal basis. Later, you may be able to get help when you need it by using individuals as independent contractors, by hiring outside vendors, or by using a temporary-help agency. Sooner or later, though, as your self-imposed duties take up more and more time, you will think of hiring help.

To Hire or Not to Hire

It is tempting to "do everything myself." After all, who knows better than you how everything should be done? Be careful, though, about getting bogged down in details that others could do as well—or better. Who is doing the promotion and sales work while you're sweeping the floor, packing cartons, answering the phone? It is probable that many entrepreneurs wait too long to hire assistants. When there seem to be too few hours in the day or too few days in the week to get things done, you will find yourself looking for helpers.

You may begin with a part-time assistant; later you may have a crew working for you—then several crews, depending on how much the business grows and how much you want it to grow. Some people are happier working with one or two trusted "old hands." Even so, as soon as you hire any employees, you need to apply some well-tested management principles. Otherwise you may have a mob instead of a team.

Remember that hiring even one employee entails certain legal and tax obligations. That is one reason some businesses utilize temporary-help agencies, especially for short-term needs. Workers supplied by such agencies are the employees of the temporary help service; you pay a specified fee for their services and incur no employer obligations.

YOUR PAYROLL TAX RESPONSIBILITIES

Federal Employer Identification Number. The IRS requires businesses to have this; you will need it in filing your federal employee tax returns. Contact the IRS and request Form SS-4. You will also need a supply of Form W-4 for employees.

Wage and Hour Regulations. Both federal and state governments specify minimum wages, hours different classes of employees may work, overtime pay, and so forth. Contact your state's department of labor and industry.

Federal Taxes. The federal government requires that federal wage tax (F.W.T.) and social security taxes (F.I.C.A.) be withheld from employees' wages. These sums are the employees' money, which you hold in trust and remit to the government at specified intervals. You must contribute an equal amount to F.I.C.A.; the tax rate and the amount of wages to which the tax is applicable change periodically. Contact the IRS and obtain Circular E.

State and Local Taxes. If your state and/or city has an income or wage tax, you will have to withhold that also. Contact the appropriate state and local agencies for information and forms (look in the telephone book under the name of your state and your city).

Self-Employment Tax. You must pay a federal self-employment tax (social security) and you must also file estimated income tax payments every quarter. Check with the IRS.

Unemployment Taxes. For federal regulations, contact the IRS. State laws vary. Obtain information from your state's department of employment security.

Disability Tax. Again, state laws and regulations vary. In some states this tax is handled by the department of employment security, in others by different departments.

Workers' Compensation. Employers must carry insurance to compensate employees for work-related injuries and/or illnesses. Regulations vary; some states provide the insurance, in others private carriers do.

"Relativity" and Your Small Business

Small-business owners often rely on relatives for their staff. Hiring relatives just because they are relatives is called **nepotism,** a term that dates back to when kings and queens appointed their nephews to government posts. Sometimes having relatives working for you benefits you and your business. Your spouse or kin may have a deeper commitment to the business than others would. However, hiring relatives can lead to friction, too. And it is harder to fire a relative than a nonrelated employee, since the stresses will affect you in your personal life. Try to evaluate your relatives as you would any "outside" applicant: Is this person the best-qualified for the job?

Orienting New Employees

Once you have hired the best available person for the job, you need to make clear what the job consists of and what your expectations are. The new employee should be clearly told whom to report to—that is, who his or her immediate superior is. Similarly, subordinates should be introduced and the lines of authority made clear.

Inexperienced managers tend to leave employees with too many assumptions and no clear statement of whose orders they should follow. Friction between employees may follow, and everyone's work will suffer. You should also clarify the rank of the new employee to others in the organization. Everyone needs to know who is in charge.

In many organizations, new members are simply told in general terms, what their duties are. ("I want you to handle the paperwork.") It is far better to write a detailed **job description,** a list of duties and responsibilities both you and the employee can refer to. The job description is best written *before* you begin seeking applicants so that you will have a clear idea of the qualifications you require, the amount of salary you can pay, the chances for advancement, and other matters.

A SAMPLE JOB DESCRIPTION

Job Title: Accountant
General Description: Maintains complete, accurate, and timely reports of all business transactions.
Specific Duties: Journal entries, posting to ledger, trial balance, quarterly and annual reports, analysis of balance sheet and operating statement, payroll, state and federal tax reports.
Reports to: Controller
Supervises: Assistant bookkeeper

Delegating Your Work to Others

Delegation consists of passing a task or a portion of a task to subordinates. It involves explaining what is to be done and holding the subordinate responsible for completing the tasks.

Entrepreneurial personalities often have problems with delegation. ("I can do it better." "It takes less time to do it than to explain it." "They'll mess it up.") If you want your business to grow, however, you will have to learn to delegate.

A common method of delegating tasks is on-job training, showing an assistant the work the way you do it. An alternative is to explain the expected outcome and leave the details to your subordinate. This method gives your subordinate an opportunity to be creative. It increases motivation and helps establish trust. And it may increase your organizational effectiveness through new, perhaps better, methods.

The Principle of Specialization

Once you decide you need help in running your business, you need to examine your activities and decide which ones can be delegated to someone else. Assigning little pieces of all your tasks to someone else is not a good idea. Instead, you need to apply the **principle of specialization:** assigning all work of one type to one person, all work of another type to a different person. Concentrating on a single activity allows a worker to become expert in that activity, leading to skill, speed, and the development of new methods and techniques for doing things.

The principle of specialization does *not* imply that you should pay no attention to whether a job has been done once you have assigned it. Even if you have "no head for figures" and your partner is "all thumbs" in the machine shop, each of you needs to be aware of what the other is doing.

BLANCHE'S DREAM WENT UP IN SMOKE

"I'm hopeless with figures," Blanche told Lisa when they opened a craft shop together. "You take care of the paperwork and all that nitty-gritty; I'll give the craft lessons—we can both buy merchandise." Lisa agreed. The business grew fast. With Thanksgiving and Christmas on the horizon, the partners ordered large lots of silk flowers, dried grasses—all the makings for wreaths, ornaments, and decorations. The shop was crammed to bursting when a careless customer dropped a cigarette into some dried wheat, setting off a fire that burned the shop and all its stock.

"We've got to get a move on," said Blanche, "and get the insurance company to settle in time for us to order in new stock."

"Insurance???" said Lisa. Lisa had forgotten to renew the policy—and Blanche had just dropped the reminders on Lisa's desk without following them up.

The Buck Still Stops with You

Remember that assigning tasks to subordinates does not relieve you of the ultimate responsibility for getting the task done. You will need to check on progress and performance—especially when a subordinate is new to a given task. Did Jean check prices from linen suppliers as you asked her to? Did she make a list of pros and cons of going with a new supplier? Has she evaluated the information and made a recommendation? Once the decision was made, did she follow through? If no linens—or two deliveries of linens—arrive on the usual day, the problem is yours as well as Jean's.

Responsibility Requires Authority

Simply delegating responsibility is not enough. With responsibility must go the authority to accomplish the job. By conveying authority in equal measure with responsibility, you are following the **principle of parity.** Often the job title and description confer authority: a foreman has authority to give instruction to shop workers, a sales manager has authority to supervise salespeople. At other times, authority rests in the freedom to make decisions, to sign purchase orders or checks, or in some other act that is needed to complete an assigned task.

How Many Is Too Many?

How many people can one person supervise effectively? At what point do you stop being "the" manager and start supervising other managers who in turn supervise other employees? The average small business has seven employees, and you may be able to supervise that many yourself. Once you have ten employees or more, however, it is unlikely that you can effectively supervise them all. Typically, seven or eight subordinates is the limit for effective supervision. When your organization reaches that size, it's time to divide the group in two and hire an assistant manager or supervisor.

The Principle of Departmentation

In Chapter 7, we talked about forming departments. Sometimes this occurs informally and almost automatically by function. Office and clerical functions become one department, production or sales become the other. As the organization becomes larger, some principle of forming departments needs to evolve. To review, the main alternatives are:

○ By function: sales, production, accounting
○ By time: day and night shifts, weekdays and weekends, full-time and part-time
○ By product
○ By territory
○ By type of customer: retail and wholesale, male and female (for certain retail businesses)

Departmental growth should be balanced. Is the sales department growing so fast that the service department is overwhelmed? Is production increasing beyond the ability of the bookkeeping department to cope? Have more advertising people been hired, and is the sales force lagging behind?

Your Organizational Chart

To help in assigning responsibilities and evaluating the lines of communication and authority in your business, you can use an organizational chart. An **organiza-** **tional chart** is a graphical depiction of the structure of a business. Vertical lines show who is subordinate to whom, which employees are in line positions and which are in staff positions.

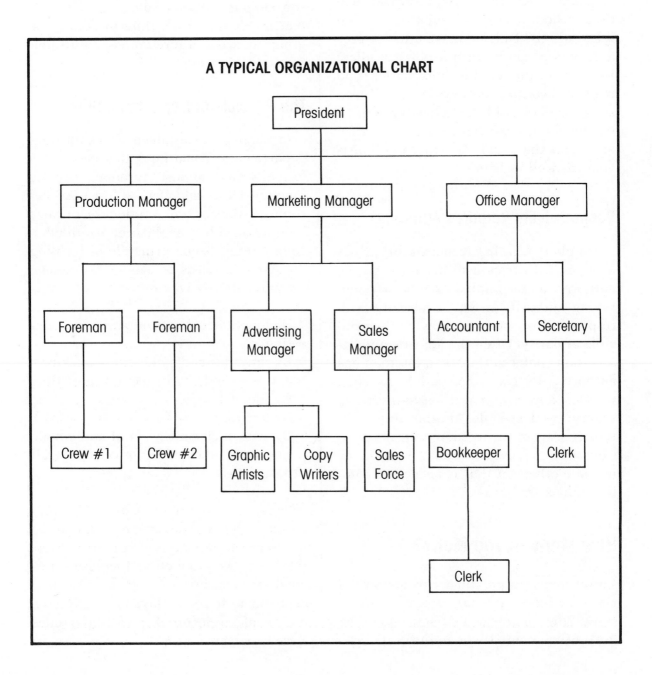

A TYPICAL ORGANIZATIONAL CHART

President

Production Manager — Marketing Manager — Office Manager

Foreman — Foreman — Advertising Manager — Sales Manager — Accountant — Secretary

Crew #1 — Crew #2 — Graphic Artists — Copy Writers — Sales Force — Bookkeeper — Clerk

Clerk

Line versus Staff Positions

A **staff worker** is a specialist who may give expert advice or suggestions but does not give orders or make decisions that affect the organization as a whole. For example, a quality-control inspector or a human resources (personnel) manager does not have the power to command others in the business. On the organizational chart, a staff worker's position is shown out to the side, not connected to any subordinates by authority lines. Management must clearly inform line workers that staff employees are advisers, not commanders. Staff positions are more common in organizations considerably larger than in the typical small business.

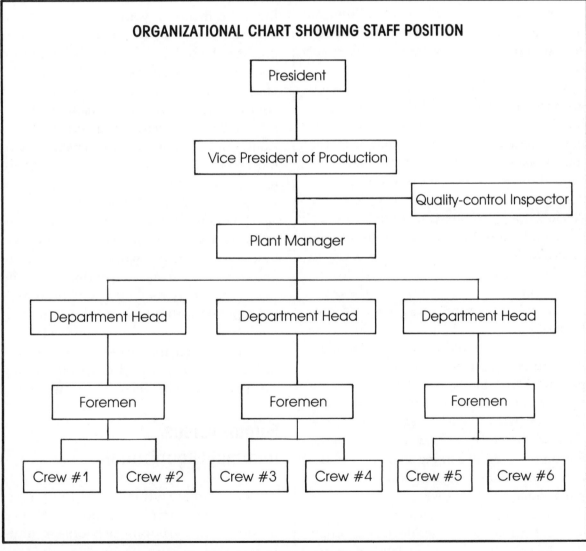

This organizational chart shows Quality-control inspector as a staff position.

Line employees hold positions at different levels of authority, supervising subordinates in their departments or in broader organizational subdivisions.

Unity of Command

Conflicting or vacillating managers confuse and frustrate their employees. This situation is likely to occur when department heads have somewhat differing opinions and their subordinates hear both views, not knowing which to follow. As manager, you are responsible for making sure that directives display a singleness of purpose.

Akin to problems of unity of command are those of dual subordination. Suppose both the plant manager and the warehouse manager are put in charge of the maintenance supervisor. Or suppose that both the bookkeeper and the office manager are authorized to give orders to the clerical staff. No one can serve two masters, and dual subordination should be avoided. They are most likely to occur in businesses that "just grow," with no attention being given to clarifying the organizational structure and lines of authority.

The organizational chart can also clarify company communications and identify potential trouble spots. Who needs to know what? Are service personnel notified about changes in parts requirements? If the sales manager in an auto agency plans a promotion emphasizing service or offering service coupons, did someone let the parts department know?

In deciding who needs to know, remember that employees are made uneasy when they feel that management is keeping secrets. Use bulletin boards, memos, newsletters, and the simple method of talking with employees to distribute and collect information.

Centralized versus Decentralized Decision Making

Is every decision made at the top? If so, your organization is centralized. This method would seem to keep the controlling reins firmly in your hands, but it can work against you, too. If every decision must be cleared with you, what happens if you are not available? Will people be afraid to make any decisions, and will your business be paralyzed as a result?

In a decentralized organization, decisions can be made at lower levels, where most of the relevant information is likely to be available. Leaving lower-level workers out of the decision-making process—which often accompanies management secrecy and distrust of subordinates—jeopardizes worker cooperation and tends to foster resentment. ("The management treats us like mushrooms—it keeps us in the dark and feeds us manure.")

If centralized management is like dictatorship, decentralized decision making can resemble, not democracy but chaos.

Formal versus Informal Organization

Formal organization is the grouping of people by design; informal organization is the unplanned grouping of people by affinity, a common purpose, or a specific task.

The formal organization can be charted; informal relationships shift and change, come and go. Most businesses have and need both kinds. If the real lines of communication and authority are not those on the chart, however, you may have less control of your business than you think you do. Try to observe and make use of the informal alliances and networks that spring up in any group of people.

Who Will Succeed You If You Get Sick or Die?

Many small entrepreneurs overlook the issue of succession. Consequently their businesses founder and fail if they suddenly become disabled or die. Training a successor can ensure that your business will outlive you.

GALLAGHER'S PRINCIPLES OF EFFECTIVE ORGANIZATION

- Formulate and distribute clear written objectives.
- Put experts in charge of departments.
- Eliminate nepotism and favoritism.
- Delegate decisions to the lowest reasonable level.
- Provide for unity of command.
- Pinpoint accountability for each task.
- Avoid spreading management too thin; keep the span at reasonable width.
- Avoid dual subordination.
- Centralize control while decentralizing decision making.
- Provide for organizational balance.
- Create results-oriented job descriptions.
- Update clear company policies and update them regularly.
- Allow flexibility in the informal organization and acknowledge the informal organization.
- Integrate personal goals—yours and your employees'—with the organization's goals.
- Provide for succession.

CHAPTER NINE

Developing Your Marketing Plan

KEY TERMS

channel of distribution	demographics	markup
cost plus calculation	the Four P's	net revenue marginal analysis
cost/volume/profit analysis	marketing	price history

So far, you have been concerned with borrowing and spending money. Now it is time to consider plans for *earning* money. Beginners in small business often neglect this aspect of planning. They tend to assume that if they do everything else right, customers will appear. But it is not enough to rent a location, purchase fixtures and equipment, organize and manage operations. Without customers, these efforts are meaningless. It is not enough to offer a product or service that *you* find attractive. For your business to succeed, people must decide to spend their money with you—to become customers. It is your responsibility to make that happen.

THE MOST COMMON MARKETING TRAPS

○ Failing to consider customers' needs and tastes more important than one's own
○ Failing to appraise the marketplace for real numbers of potential customers
○ Failing to interview customers and ask their honest opinion of a product before purchasing large quantities for sale
○ Failing to consider the true size of the target market: people who have a strong need for a product (of the total number of computer owners, how many would actually buy an antistatic brush?)
○ Failing to appreciate the size and effectiveness of the competition
○ Failing to try a new product while sales of an existing product are high
○ Failing to try a new marketing approach while sales are satisfactory
○ Failing to notice market trends that will lead to reduced business (some shoe-repair operators failed to notice that shoes were becoming disposable products)
○ Failing to investigate additional uses for one's product. (When Mother stopped baking cakes from scratch, Arm & Hammer was ready with baking-soda cat litter, rug cleaner, detergent, and many other products, all packaged for instant recognition of the company's identity.)

What Is Marketing?

Marketing is not just selling, or advertising, or putting goods on display. It is a little of each—and more. **Marketing** consists of all activities that encourage goods and services to flow from those who produce them to those who consume them. Marketing is neither producing goods and services nor consuming them—but it is everything else that fosters trade and commerce: salesmanship, display, merchandising, packaging, advertising, promotion, price discounts, coupon deals and giveaways, banners, posters, printed coffee mugs, fairs and festivals, sidewalk sales and clearance sales, Mother's Day and Christmas.

Marketing is the whole process of having the right product, at the right time, in the right place, calling attention to it and thereby bringing a mutual benefit to customer and vendor. Customers benefit by having what they want when and where they want it—freshly squeezed orange juice at the 7-Eleven instead of oranges on a tree a thousand miles away. Vendors benefit by making a profit. The greater the benefits customers perceive, the more frequently they will trade with the businesses that provide them.

You are engaging in marketing when you:
○ Design or develop a product or service
○ Transport and store goods
○ Provide a variety of choice

○ Buy in large volumes and sell item by item
○ Install, service, repair, instruct
○ Update and improve

Marketing is providing a customer hotline, staying open until midnight or on Sundays, adding a measuring cap to a detergent container, processing food in "singles" sizes. Marketing is the **Four P's:** The product, the place, the price, and the promotion. But most of all, marketing is research: finding out who the customers are and what they need. Successful vendors never forget that *benefit lies in the customer's perception*, not in the vendor's.

Marketing is asking the question, "Who will buy my product or service?"

Finding Your Target Market

Not everyone is your potential customer. There is no product or service that everyone buys in the same form and at the same time. Don't make the mistake of thinking that people are identical, and that marketing consists simply of selling to the largest possible percentage of the general population. People have widely differing tastes—in food, in music, in clothing, in cars, in how they spend their time. Some will be too young to use your product or service even indirectly; some will be too old; some will already have it, and so on. People who can't read won't buy from your bookstore, and people who hate rock music won't patronize a lounge where it is played.

It is your job to identify a target market. Without knowing what it is and how large it is, you cannot know whether your busi-

ness is feasible. And without continued market research, you can't truly identify your product or make a profit. It's not enough say, "I'll sell clothing." If you tried to suit everyone, you would have to open a combination of Saks, Sears, the local outlet store, a boutique, a costume shop, and a thrift shop. Even the largest department stores are more selective than that.

Suppose you want to sell boats and marine supplies. "Boats" encompasses yachts, rowboats, canoes, iceboats, kayaks, white-water rafts, build-it-yourself sailboat kits, and life rafts—not to speak of aircraft carriers, submarines, and ocean liners. Narrow your potential market down to people who wish to sail on a large nearby lake. Then, select subgroups: first-time boat owners, families with children, and people who take boating seriously enough to race their boats. Now your target customers are those looking for three kinds of products: inexpensive boats for beginners, larger boats designed for families, and racing models. Even this may be too broad a market, and you may want to narrow it down even further.

If you are planning a hardware and building supply business, consider whether you are targeting do-it-yourselfers or professional contractors. What merchandise would each type of customer want? What sort of salespeople? Do-it-yourselfers want lots of advice, and perhaps a selection of rental tools. Professionals want to get in and out in a hurry.

Using Demographics

Use **demographic statistics** to help target your market. Demography is more than head counting; it is the study of the characteristics of a population—age, income, occupation, mobility, and so on. This topic was already discussed at some length in relation to your business plan; now consider it in terms of your general business plan. Now, consult your local Chamber of Commerce, the sales representatives at the local radio and TV stations, your local newspaper, your librarian, and some real estate people. Radio and newspaper advertising staffs are especially well acquainted with the demographics of their trading area.

Your marketing effort should be focused on a target group as specific as you can make it. Even the largest businesses do this. McDonald's, for example, initially targeted families with young children. No pinball machines or similar distractions were permitted. Now, after several decades of doing business with these target customers, McDonald's has a whole new, additional set of target customers: people to whom McDonald's—once the newest of concepts—has nostalgia value and tradition because they went there as children.

Defining What Your Target Market Wants

Once you have established a target market and a general type of business, zero in. Ask yourself, "What do my customers *re-*

TONY MISSED THE TARGET

"This place could be a gold mine," thought Tony. The owner of the neighborhood bar and grill was retiring, and the price he was asking seemed low. "With a little sprucing up, I'll soon have every table filled," thought Tony. The blue-collar customers seemed to like the place. Each time Tony came in, a fair-sized group of them were gathered around the TV, drinking beer, eating, joking, placing private bets on the game. "These will be my core customers," Tony thought. He put in booths, new lighting, a salad bar, a larger TV. But after the Grand Opening, business started to fall off. New customers were slow in coming—the shabby neighborhood didn't appeal to them. The restaurant had no parking area—most of the trade had been walk-ins. And many of the old customers stopped coming. Too late, Tony did some market research and found out that the shabby, homey, casual look was what had been bringing the customers in. With the new decor, and with "Pops" no longer behind the bar, "The place ain't the same." Tony has missed the target.

ally want?" Here you need to exercise some empathy. It's true that people won't come to your boat store unless they want a boat—or think they might want one in the future. People don't come to a bank unless they have some kind of money business to transact. At that point, why do they choose one bank and not another? One restaurant and not another?

Maybe they want to be able to bank/eat/shop before or after work or on weekends. If so, they will choose an establishment that is open beyond 9 to 5. Maybe they want to bank/eat/shop without getting dressed up or leaving their cars. They will look for drive-in facilities.

Maybe they want to be able to bring their children along, or their Seeing Eye dog. Maybe they want to be able to shop from a wheelchair.

You can be sure that customers want service—not just lip service. They do not want to have to wait three weeks for an appointment to have the oil changed . . . or to take time off from work to have the car serviced . . . or to return three times for the same repair. And they do not want to hear about your problems ("The delivery was late"; "We're two mechanics short"; "The company sent the wrong part"). They do not want the "Counter Closed" sign put up on the dot of five when they've been waiting in line for half an hour.

If you can address and rectify such common consumer complaints, you will be creating customer satisfaction. That is the true basis of effective marketing.

Successful marketing means being in touch with your customers, being sensitive to their needs. To do that, you need to know all about them. What will make them get up from the couch, leave the TV, put on their shoes, drive in traffic to your location, put money in the parking meter, use their valuable time to deal with you, and part with their money? That's a tall order. It takes a major effort to make people change their habits, to turn into a new traffic pattern. To do that, you need a strong, persuasive combination of the Four P's of marketing: product, place, price, and promotion.

Product: The First "P"

What are you selling? Be sure you know. It's bound to be more than the specific item or service you have for sale. McDonald's sells more than meat on a bun. They deliver a predictable product, quality and portion control, fast service, protective packaging, spill-proof beverage containers, and food when you want it—no reservations required. Effective marketing does not sell goods; it sells customer satisfactions. The larger the bundle of satisfactions you can deliver, the more successful you will be.

Establishing Your Business Identity

Consumers not only need to know what you sell, they need to know that *you* are selling it. The bundle of satisfactions you are selling needs to be clearly identified as yours—with a strong suggestion that it's yours alone. Whether your business is large or small, you can brand it as yours with the right combination of words, pictures, and packaging.

WHAT SHOULD I CALL MY BUSINESS?

It's tempting to name your business after yourself: Tony's Place . . . Mario's . . . Gallagher's. The problem is that by itself, your name gives no clue to what business you're in. Other entrepreneurs come up with clever formulations: Trixamatic . . . Savon/Costs . . . Klearview. Many of these names also leave the nature of the business a mystery.

Sometimes a personal name plus the name of the product or service will work, especially if the business is one in which people like to know who the proprietor is: Speedy's Sporting Goods . . . Ellen's Styling Salon.

Try to combine the two concepts without being mysterious. Only major corporations can afford generic names like USX, Citicorp, or VISA. Try alliteration (repetition of the first sound in a word) for a catchy name: The two T's in "Tutor/Tape" make the name easy to remember and say. "Well-Done Welding" might work better than "Santino's Auto Body and Fender Repair Shop"; "Sandy's Candies" is more memorable than "Johnson's Delectables."

Try to relate your name to a specific customer need: "Hometown Delivery Service"; "Greenlawn Landscaping"; "Healthaerobics." Keep your image in mind, too. For example, "Sandy's Candies" has a less formal sound than "Johnson's Delectables"; for that very reason it may have less appeal to customers looking for a gourmet product with luxurious packaging.

If your name is the same as or close to that of a famous business, be cautious about using it. Don't call your restaurant "McDonald's" even if that is your name.

A "package" is more than a carton or a wrapper. It is your total presentation of yourself and your product. To achieve a package that sells, you need to keep your name constantly before the public. Your business name should be on your building—the front door, the rear door, the counters, on your vehicles, on your goods. Invest a few hundred dollars in a well-designed logo, or logotype. Then use it everywhere.

Your logo says a lot about your business; it conveys a pictorial image that should tie in with the concept of your business you want the public to visualize. Think of the difference in image conveyed by IBM and Apple computers. IBM uses a precise, almost geometric rendering of its corporate initials. Apple uses a stylized apple with a bite taken out of it. What do these two logos tell you about each company's approach?

As time passes, your business packaging may need revitalizing. Find a book on trademarks at the library and compare logos from thirty or fifty years ago to those used by the same company today. Look at the trademarks of Coca-Cola, Kellogg, and other giants. Look at the symbol used by the phone company to indicate the presence of a pay phone. How are these the same over the years? How have they changed?

As you package your product or service, keep in mind the different markets and submarkets at which it might be aimed. Are you selling to industrial customers? The military? Or to consumers.

Industrial Products and Services

Some products are sold to industry, not to individual customers. Industrial products include rivets, adhesives, machine tools, component parts, commercial fixtures, and so on. If your product or service is designed for industrial use, you will be marketing it to lists of client industries such as food processors, steel mills, electronics plants, or clothing factories. You can find these clients through such publications as the *Thomas Register*, available at libraries, and the mailing lists of trade organizations and periodicals. In marketing industrial products and services, you will be focusing on specifications, dimensions, blueprints, and technical details. Industrial customers want easy installation, on-site training of their workers, low cost, and reliability.

Military Products

Do not overlook the military as potential customers. The U.S. government spends billions on defense-related products and services, not all of it with large companies. To reach this market, you will have to pursue requests for bids (often listed in the newspapers), make presentations to military procurement officers, and maintain contacts at military bases. Testing and reliability are stressed. The paperwork requirements may confound you; you may want to use sales agents who specialize in military procurement.

Consumer Products and Services

Most small businesses market to consumers, the end users of their product or service. Consumer goods fall into several classifications, which in turn are based on consumer perceptions. One person's impulse item is another person's emergency purchase.

Impulse Goods. What kinds of things do you buy on the spur of the moment? Souvenirs, novelties, toys, gadgets, luxuries? Impulse goods are not on the shopping list; they must have instant appeal. Toothpaste is a staple; an electric toothbrush may be an impulse purchase.

To market impulse goods, you must price them low enough so that people will not hesitate to buy them. (The actual price will depend on the economic status of your potential customers; for some, $5 may be too much; for others, $50 may be just right.) You must place the product or advertise the service where it will be noticed and display it prominently and appealingly. A "teddy bear tree" near the cash register works well for one candy store (candy itself tends to be an impulse item). The item must have high novelty appeal; impulse items are often fad merchandise and must be sold while the fad is "hot."

Shopping Goods. Cars, boats, VCRs, and winter coats are examples of shopping goods. They usually cost a large portion of the budget, are infrequently purchased, and require comparison shopping for price and value. Remember what was said about compatibility when you sell shopping goods; locate near your competitors so that shoppers will include you among the businesses whose products are being compared. In marketing shopping goods, price is a consideration, but so are performance, durability, serviceability, and similar attributes.

Specialty Goods. These products or services are unique, highly in demand, and with few substitutes or none. Parts for a specific brand of photocopier, a patented tool, custom-made draperies or clothing are all specialty goods. Are you selling a product or service that people will go out of their way to purchase? If so, you will emphasize uniqueness and availability rather than price or convenience of location.

Emergency Goods. Consumers do little or no shopping for auto towing, crutch or wheelchair rentals, or emergency repairs. They may accept what is offered because circumstances of time or place offer no effective competition. (Consumers do remember being gouged, however.) In marketing such items, you need most of all to let people know where to find them.

Convenience Goods. Consumers shopping for bread, milk, newspapers, cigarettes, and candy do not want to travel long distances to get them; they do not compare prices or look for discounts be-cause convenience is the important thing. Selection is less important than with other products. When you market fast food, disposable tableware, and many other products, the convenience it offers is part of the product package.

Place: The Second "P"

In Chapter 3, the issue of location was addressed mainly from the standpoint of customer traffic. Other considerations also count. Where will you store your inventory (supplies)? Where will they be coming from—that is, where are your main suppliers located? How fast can you get goods, and how fast can you deliver your product or service? "Place" includes such matters as taking customers' orders and having them "drop-shipped" directly from the manufacturer; stocking goods on the customers' premises; using public warehouses; storing inventory in tractor trailers or mobile storage units.

You need to consider shipping costs and timing your ordering and shipping to meet peak demands (refrigerators and air conditioners tend to break down in summer, automobiles in winter—affecting both sales and service demand). You need to think about the risk of deterioration (great if you are selling fish, small if you are selling nuts and bolts) and the risk that stored goods will become obsolete before you can sell them (a problem with seasonal goods and impulse merchandise). Taken together, all these factors relate to your **channel of distribution:** the means by which your product or service reaches its users. The channel of distribution includes purchasing and sales, transportation and delivery, warehousing and storage, risk taking, financing, insurance, and credit.

Who will bear financial risks: You? The manufacturer? The consumer? Who pays for transportation? Insurance? Packaging? Freight? (Ultimately, the consumer pays for all these things, but you must decide whether the payment will be direct or indirect, and what form it will take.)

Within the channel of distribution are agent middlemen, brokers, selling agents, manufacturing agents, auctioneers, drop shippers, wagon jobbers, rack jobbers, importers and exporters, and bulk stations. Which of these facilities you will use depends on such considerations as your need to use others' capital, the perishability of the goods, the speed of delivery you need, the service you or the customers expect, and where you and your customer are located. You must choose the channel of distribution that costs least within the constraints of service and time.

Another consideration for retail stores is the nature of the business enterprise. Is your business a single unit or a chain? Are you carrying goods from a single manufacturer (for example, one brand of shoes) or from many? Are you selling one category of item (for example, leather goods or ice cream) or a wide variety? A department store carries many kinds of goods from many places; a discount store does also, at reduced prices. A franchise business offers recognized goods under a well-known name in a standardized manner that generally extends to store layout and choice of suppliers.

You might also consider vending—that is, selling merchandise through coin-operated machines. Even insurance policies and package delivery have been sold through vending machines. In such instances you need to determine how the machines will be supplied and resupplied with goods, who will repair them, and how the money will be collected.

Price: The Third "P"

How do you determine the selling price for your product or service? How can you know whether you are charging too much or too little? Break-even analysis has already been discussed, but this technique merely tells you how many units you must sell or how many dollars you must take in before you start making a profit. You can bring in more dollars by raising prices—but raising prices will also reduce sales. This problem is especially likely to occur if customers perceive your prices as exorbitant—much higher than what other businesses are charging for the same thing.

In determining your prices, remember that consumers do not buy price—they react to *value*. If they do not perceive that they will receive value for their money, they will not buy from you.

Factors That Affect Price

Every firm operates within the constraints of its **price history.** If your business is known for selling bargain goods or inexpensive merchandise, you may find it hard to sell high-priced goods. Conversely, if you are known for luxury goods, few customers will come to you for bargain merchandise. Some businesses emphasize being first with the newest—the first

VCRs, the first large-screen TVs. They may be able to skim the cream off the market by charging high prices; once the product becomes commonplace, customers are likely to go elsewhere. For example, when personal computers first came into use, diskettes for data storage were sold at computer stores at prices of as high as $10 apiece. Today they are available at K Mart and Best at $1 each and less.

Neighborhood also determines "what the traffic will bear," although the idea that you can sell cheaply in a poor neighborhood may be erroneous. In such neighborhoods your insurance costs may be higher, your losses from vandalism and pilferage may be greater, and so on.

Demand always determines price; however, demand may fluctuate with the season, the fashion, or the location. Thus, price depends on timing; it also depends on competition. More people purchase gasoline just before a major holiday and on weekends; the price may go up at such times. More people buy film and developing services at Christmas and other holidays; prices may go up accordingly—or at least no sales will be held at such times. Merchants in seasonal resorts must price their goods to compensate for the months when business is slow or nonexistent.

Methods of Determining Selling Price

One common method of arriving at a selling price is called **cost plus.** You determine what an item costs you, then add a percentage for operating expenses and overhead. Thus, if you determine that you need to add a 60 percent markup to cover

your selling cost plus your profit, you sell an item that costs you $1 for $1.60 and an item that costs you $10 for $16. Many retailers determine their operating margin and then set their prices so as to maintain a given percentage of markup, either on individual items or as an average.

Another way to calculate prices is the **cost/volume/profit analysis.** This method helps you predict the effect of price on the number of sales and calculate the point at which these factors combine to give you the best profit. Your estimate of volume may come from intuition or from market research done for similar products. The calculation formula is:

$$P = \text{price}$$
$$Q = \text{quantity}$$
$$R = \text{revenue}$$
$$C = \text{cost of goods}$$
$$PR = \text{profit}$$
and
$$P \times Q = R - C = PR$$

Suppose you are selling hamburgers that cost you 90 cents. You make the calculation at various volumes and prices to determine the optimum volume and price:

$$\$1.00 \times 500 = \$500 - \$450 = \$\ 50$$
$$\$1.25 \times 400 = \$500 - \$360 = \$140$$
$$\$1.50 \times 200 = \$300 - \$180 = \$120$$
$$\$1.90 \times 100 = \$190 - \$\ 90 = \$\ 90$$

Your best selling price for this product alone is $1.25. Of course, you would probably be selling french fries and beverages, too, at the very least, and the prices for these items would enter into your final determinations.

A method called **net revenue marginal analysis** carries this method a step farther. This cost-setting system determines the last item sold. That price is often lower than that charged for items sold previously. For example, a theater manager finds that offering movie tickets at $5 yields only 80 percent occupancy. Since the show must run anyway, offering tickets at $1 to passersby just before show time will increase profits.

Or, you have been selling strawberries at the farmers' market all day at $2. When it is nearly closing time you have ten baskets left. They will spoil by tomorrow, and you will have to store them overnight or take them home. You may start offering them at two for $3, then $1 each, and finally two for $1. Covering your cost of goods sold plus a penny of overhead is better than earning no revenue at all toward your overhead.

How to Calculate Your Markup

Your **markup** is the percentage of difference between your cost for a product or service and its selling price. For a product, markup is generally figured on the wholesale price. For a service, markup may be figured on labor cost per hour. Markup must include your overhead as well as your profit.

There are two ways of viewing markup. *Markup on cost* is accomplished by adding a specified percentage of the cost of an item to arrive at the retail (selling) price. Suppose an item costs you $10. You decide to add a markup of 100 percent of cost— $10—and arrive at a selling price of $20.

Markup on retail views the same calculation from the opposite perspective. By adding $10 to an item that cost you $10, you have arrived at a markup from retail of 50 percent, meaning that if you discounted the retail selling price of $20 by 50 percent, you would arrive at $10. By custom, most retailers simply refer to a 100 percent markup on cost as "a 50 percent markup," with "on retail" being understood.

Steps in Your Marketing Plan

Formulating your marketing plan consists of a series of steps. At each point, be sure that you have answered every question in as much detail as possible. Together, all the answers to all the questions should provide you with a plan that you can follow up with specific strategies discussed in Chapter 10.

First, Define Your Business

○ What is my business in general terms— that is, what customer needs will I be filling?
○ What are the geographical limits of my marketing area: national, regional, local, or neighborhood?
○ Who are my competitors? What are their strengths and weaknesses?
○ How does my business differ from the competition?
○ Why should customers do business with me instead of my competition?

Second, Define Your Customers

○ What is my customers' age, sex, income, occupation, homeownership status, ethnic background? What are their interests and tastes?

○ Which of my customers' habits and patterns of behavior are relevant to my business?

○ How do I expect my customers to learn about my products and services?

○ Where do my customers buy these items now? What do they read and listen to? How can I get them to come to me?

○ Who has a need for my product or service that I am currently not reaching?

Define Your Marketing Plan

○ What marketing methods do I expect to use to reach my customers? What methods are others using successfully?

○ Which strategies would be most effective in reaching my particular customers? What are the steps of those strategies?

○ What is the value to me of one new customer?

○ How often will one new customer buy from me in a year?

○ How much will he or she spend?

○ How much am I willing to spend to get one new customer?

○ What profit can I expect from one customer in one year?

○ What am I doing to keep my old customers? Am I ignoring them in the search for new ones?

○ How many customers do I need to satisfy my revenue goals?

○ What percentage of my revenues should I spend on marketing?

○ What marketing tools (sales personnel, TV ads, outdoor signs, and so on—see Chapter 10) can I implement within my budget?

○ How can I test my ideas in the market without spending all my marketing dollars?

○ How can I verify that my marketing efforts are getting results?

○ What new ways can I think of to market my business?

When you have completed your broad marketing plan, you will be ready to tackle the fourth "P": promotion.

CHAPTER TEN

Promoting Your Business

KEY TERMS

advertising	*graphic design*	*public relations*
A.I.D.A. objectives	*merchandising*	*publicity*
direct mail	*promotion*	*sales promotion*

The objectives of **promotion,** the fourth "P" of marketing, are:

○ To create public awareness of your business and its products and services
○ To stimulate desire for your products and services
○ To bring customers to your business

You will then have to apply salesmanship (Chapter 11) to persuade them to buy.

The A.I.D.A. Objectives

Promotion is more than advertising, although advertising is part of it. Promotion consists of all the activities you use to create:

○ Attention—Capture customers' attention
○ Interest—Awaken their interest
○ Desire—Stimulate their desire to buy
○ Action—Move them to action

The A.I.D.A. objectives are central to all promotional activities.

Beginners tend to overlook these objectives. They allocate scarce advertising dollars ineffectively, using techniques and media that bring them no results. They jump blindly into radio spots, newspaper ads, or listings in the Yellow Pages without giving enough thought to the return they will get for each dollar spent.

Promotion begins with knowing what your target customers read, view, listen to, attend, travel by, and encounter in their everyday lives. If your target market consists of middle-aged men who spend Sunday watching ball games on TV, you waste every dollar you spend on "slick" magazines or on ads on the back page of comic books. If you are seeking customers for impulse luxury items or gourmet catering, there is little point in advertising on bowling score pads. If you are trying to change ingrained habits, one full-page newspaper ad won't do it; your money would be better spent on smaller advertisements placed over time or even on some other promotional tool.

Analysts of advertising and promotion estimate that only 3 percent of the public are innovators, quick to try out a new product or idea. From 10 to 15 percent are early adapters; depending on the total time frame, they may try a new product within weeks or months. The early majority of 35 percent may need to be aware of a new product or a new vendor for a year before they try it. Another 35 percent will take a few years to change their trading habits. The last 5 to 15 percent are labeled laggards; whatever their reasons, they have not purchased even after most of their neighbors own a new product. Think about some product that was new recently: VCRs, portable phones, microwaves. How many of your friends and family bought these products early? How many haven't bought them yet?

One-shot or short-range promotion is likely to bring you only the innovators—and perhaps not all of those, depending on how unique your product is. Is that all you want to shoot for?

Your promotional efforts must be well rounded and well targeted. They should include all aspects of promotion that are applicable to your business, whether they consist of advertising, direct mail, sales promotion, publicity, public relations, or personal selling.

Advertising

Advertising is any paid communication by an identified sponsor intended to cause prospects to turn toward an idea, a product, or a service. The word comes from the Latin *advert*, which means "turn toward." Advertising that is not paid for directly by the potential seller is called publicity or word of mouth.

Your advertising can be designed to inform, to educate, to remind, or to persuade. Most businesses use advertising to expand markets and generate sales, but some forms of advertising are intended mainly to create goodwill. If you buy an ad in a high school yearbook, you probably don't expect it to generate sales right away; you do hope it will make students and parents think well of you and your business.

Suiting Your Message to Your Market and Your Medium

Although the word "media" has come to mean radio and TV to most people, these electronic media are only part of a media spectrum that includes print media (newspapers and magazines), billboards and posters, and specialty advertising ranging from blimps to sandwich boards. Before you select an advertising medium, you should consider the audience you want to reach.

Suppose you want to sell lawnmowers. Your target market is homeowners with lawns. Television, besides being expensive, would waste your message on many people who are not part of your target market—apartment dwellers. Radio, on the other hand, reaches commuters at certain times of the day, and people who drive cars may also own homes and lawns. You think further and realize that the best time to persuade homeowners to buy lawnmowers would be when they are thinking about their lawns—when they're homeward bound, perhaps on a Friday evening. If you are going to use radio, you need a local station with a suburban audience that will schedule your advertisement between, say, 5 and 7 P.M.

Do your customers need to see the product, or at least a picture of the product, before shopping for it? A TV picture is fleeting; radio is pictureless. If buyers need to see plans, specifications, dimensions, or working parts, a print ad would be preferable to one on radio or TV.

Consider the other habits and preferences of your target audience. Baseball and beer have a long association. Perhaps you should advertise on TV, or on the sports pages. Career training ads may do well on daytime TV, when unemployed people may be watching.

Electronic Media

Radio advertising.   Advertising by radio is affordable if you use local stations. Remember that people tend to listen to the radio when they're doing something else—driving to work, dressing, preparing meals. They may not be able to write down your name, address, and telephone number. For that reason, radio ads may be better for establishing general awareness or for calling people's attention to some other promotional activity such as a sale, an ethnic food festival, or cooking lessons.

Radio ads are easily forgotten. Also, many listeners habitually tune them out. Repetition is needed. Alliteration, musical jingles, distinctive voices, and novelty help people remember ads. Don't select a radio station just because you like it; if your target market is teenagers, money spent on an "easy listening" station is wasted.

Plan well ahead if you want to use radio for seasonal promotions. In contacting the radio station, allow at least a few weeks before you want the ad aired. Someone has to write it, you have to approve it, and the time for the ad must be scheduled, usually well in advance of when you want the ad aired.

Television advertising.   Using television is the most expensive form of advertising. Small local stations are cheaper. If your business requires a large volume and has a wide target audience, TV may work for you. Think carefully, though, about whether your promotional budget might not better be spent on a variety of less expensive forms of advertising such as print ads or circulars. If your target market is upper middle class and professional people, you might consider looking into "supporting" public television programs, which draw this kind of audience.

Print Media

The print media consist of newspapers and magazines. Both have their advertising uses.

Newspapers.   Newspaper advertising is most effective in reaching adults in towns and small cities. Perhaps 80 percent of them read newspapers. Like radio advertising, newspaper ads require repetition to be effective; studies show that six small advertisements are more effective than a single ad six times their size. When you use newspaper advertising, remember people's habits. Newspaper ads are good for about one day; after that they are discarded. Some people do clip and save newspaper ads, and this gives them an advantage over electronic media.

Display ads (those found on the news pages) are costly; classified ads are cheaper. Not all prospective customers will see them, but people who do read the classified ads are likely to be in the market for something. Some newspapers also have classified directories in which you can list your business by category: plumbing, wallpaper and paint, and so on.

Magazines.   Magazines and professional and trade journals have a long lead time; to get into the December issue you must place your ad in August or September, for example. Many magazines have classified as well as display ads, usually at cheaper rates. If you examine the magazine rack at your stationery store, you'll see a multitude of specialized magazines in addition to general-readership publications. There are magazines for cat lovers, for investors, for computer owners, for crossword puzzle addicts, for hobbyists of all kinds. In addition, there are journals for all professions and occupations. The minute a new demographic category is discovered, a magazine pops up to serve it.

Magazine ads cost more than newspaper ads, but they also last longer and are apt to be seen by more people. Besides their subscribers, they are read by patients in waiting rooms and patrons in libraries.

Because of their expense, magazine ads are best created by a professional advertising agency. Allow six weeks before the magazine's deadline for the agency to do its work. Be sure to obtain a firm price quotation before authorizing an agency to proceed with an ad.

Writing an Effective Advertisement

To be effective, an ad must first grab the reader's attention and then present a clear message. A photo or drawing or a clever headline may serve as an attention getter.

When you write the copy (the words), make every word count. Be sure your ad includes:

○ A description of what you are selling
○ The name of your business
○ The location of your business (address and directions if needed)
○ Your telephone number
○ Your hours of operation—especially if you offer evening or weekend hours
○ What you want the customer to do: call, come in, place an order
○ Instructions for ordering

These may seem self-evident, but many beginners overlook one or more points. Before you turn an ad over to be printed, ask a few strangers for their comments. You may find that your message is less clear than you supposed.

Circulars, Brochures, and Leaflets

Printed materials such as flyers and circulars are among the least costly advertising media. A local printer or graphics design firm can help you create these materials.

Designing Your Circular

Graphic design consists of all the elements that contribute to the appearance and readability of printed materials.

YOUR ADVERTISING CHECKLIST

○ Did I look at a map and outline the area from which I expect to draw my customers?
○ How do I plan to reach those customers with my advertising?
○ How much coverage will be wasted if I advertise in local newspapers?
○ Which newspapers cover this area best? Can I afford their rates?
○ What other print media could I use, such as circulars or shopping newspapers? What are their rates?
○ What radio stations cover the area? What are their rates?
○ Is there a mailing list available that covers the area? Have I checked the Yellow Pages under "Mailing Services"?
○ Should I make up my own mailing list from the phone book or a "reverse directory" (available at the library)?
○ Could I hand-distribute circulars at places where shoppers are concentrated?
○ Does my business name advertise my product or service?
○ Does my business need a sign? Will it give information about my business? Is it permitted under local ordinances?

Typefaces, pictorial materials, paper quality, and the arrangement of elements on the page make a considerable difference in the effect of any advertising piece. Most printers have some graphic design experience; more and more, graphic design is being done by independent graphics firms, usually employing computer technology. The "mechanical," or "camera-ready copy," is then taken to a printer who makes up the printing plate and prints the item.

Pictures help your sales presentation if they are clear and vivid. "Stock" drawings can also be chosen from "clip art books" offering thousands of drawings—comical, representational, old-fashioned, and so on. The typeface you select and the finish and weight of the paper influence consumer response also. Newsprint stock that works well for a tire store would be inappropriate if you are selling designer clothes or one-of-a-kind crafts.

Obtaining a Price Quotation

A general rule in printing is: The more copies you want, the cheaper each copy will be. The costs of setting up are the same whether you want 100 flyers or 100,000. In fact, the cost per item would be so great for 100 that you would be better off using press-on type or typewriting and a photocopier. Today's computerized desktop publishing systems can produce attractive materials, but putting together a truly effective piece takes experience, design sense, and skill.

○ Will my sign, my stationery, my business cards, and the lettering on my business vehicle present a consistent image of my business?

○ Have I had a logo created for use on my sign and my printed material?

○ What am I going to advertise?

○ Why should a customer come to me instead of my competition?

○ Have I set up an advertising budget for my opening and one for continuing ads?

○ Have I decided what proportion of the budget will be allocated to classified and display ads, electronic media, circulars, sales promotion?

○ Have I considered telemarketing?

○ Will the Yellow Pages work for me? What kind and size of ads is my competition running?

○ Have I sought out opportunities for publicity?

○ Have I taken or obtained good photographs of my business and my products?

○ Have I discussed my advertising plans with the staff at local newspapers, radio stations, and TV stations?

○ Have I studied newspapers, magazines, and media advertising for ideas? Have I consulted professionals?

○ Have I plotted my promotions on a large calendar and scheduled all preparatory work?

When you obtain a quotation from the printer, be sure everything is included. Generally there will be an extra charge for photographs. If you want the materials collated, folded, perforated, stapled, or otherwise prepared for distribution, specify this in advance and obtain a quotation. Last-minute changes cost money and increase errors. Have someone else proofread the copy you give to the printer; few people see their own mistakes. Be clear about what you want, since resetting type costs money.

Distributing Your Circulars

In some cases, distribution will consist simply of placing your circulars where people are likely to pick them up. Door-to-door distribution may work if you believe everyone in a neighborhood is a true target customer. Do not place circulars in mailboxes; this is against federal laws. Do not litter. Placing circulars under windshield wipers is not a good way to distribute them; it annoys many people, and you can be fined for each piece that someone throws away.

Other ways to distribute printed materials include packing one with each item you sell, putting them into customers' shopping bags, or placing them in strategic locations such as libraries (obtain permission first). You can also distribute explanatory leaflets to customers, perhaps listing special services. For a dry-cleaning business, this might be suede cleaning or fur storage; for a florist it might be plant rentals, silk arrangements, or hospital delivery. You can also include leaflets with the bills you send to customers.

Sometimes you can arrange with other merchants to distribute their circulars in return for their distributing yours.

Direct Mail

Direct mail is selling items by sending promotional materials and taking orders through the mail. It is a field all its own, with its own publications and experts. It is the fastest-growing medium in the United States. You can target your direct-mail advertising with great precision; lists are available of every imaginable target market—farmers owning small acreages, families with small children, skiers earning over $50,000 who travel by air. Mailing list houses (see Resources for this chapter) can help you zero in on potential customers whose demographic characteristics precisely match your target market.

You can purchase lists in the form of preprinted labels ready to attach to your circular. You can also type your list yourself and photocopy it onto sheets of pressure-sensitive labels, available at stationery stores. If you have a computer with a mail-merging program, you can develop your own list of customers sorted by categories (see Chapter 7).

The U.S. Postal Service offers discounts to mailers who sort their mail by ZIP code. Reduced rates are available for bulk mailings of 200 pieces or more; if you mail more than 800 pieces in a calendar year you will break even on the application fee at current rates. Inquire at your post office.

Some businesses sell entirely by mail, through catalogs. From Sears, Roebuck onward, many entrepreneurs have created mail-order empires: Lillian Vernon, L. L. Bean, and many others do all or most of their business by mail.

Calculating the Effectiveness of Your Mail Promotions

On the average, you can expect a 1 percent response from any direct-mail promotion—that is, from each 100 pieces mailed, one sale will result. This figure presupposes that you have selected an appropriate target market; some mailings garner even less response. Some very effective mailing campaigns yield a 3 percent response, but you cannot count on that much.

To calculate whether a mailing will be profitable, use the break-even analysis technique explained in Chapter 4. Suppose you were contemplating a mailing of 5,000 pieces to sell a cassette tape recorder at $90. Your total sales would be 50 recorders at $90, or $4,500. The recorders cost you $26 each, or $1,300 total. Now calculate your mailing cost:

Graphic design and printing	$ 2,000
Address labels	300
Affixing labels and sorting	200
Postal permit fee	50
Postage	450
TOTAL MAILING COST	$ 3,000

50 × $90 =	$ 4,500
Less cost of goods sold	− 1,300
Less mailing cost	− 3,000
Net profit on mailing	$ 200

If the mailing appears unprofitable, consider selling a more expensive item or reducing the cost of the mailing piece.

Sales Promotions

Sales promotions are special events—often one-day occurrences—planned to increase customer traffic. They range from Grand Opening sales to Going Out Of Business sales, manager's specials, and promotions tied in to holidays, national celebrations, the Olympics, or any other occasion that offers a promotional theme. Celebrities and fictional characters, from Darth Vader to the Tooth Fairy, may be booked to lure customers in. Sometimes promotions have an overall theme—microwave cooking, cake decoration, photography lessons. A stationery store might offer calligraphy lessons and handwriting analysis. Use your imagination.

Giveaways and premiums are often used in sales promotions: custom-printed calendars, pens, ice scrapers, paint stirrers, and more can be purchased from firms that sell advertising specialties. You can find them in the telephone book. Before you decide on a giveaway, think carefully about its value to you and to your customers. Will it really bring in new business?

It may be better to tie a giveaway in with an actual sale: a summer's worth of charcoal with every barbecue set, free serving pieces with every set of dishes, a year's subscription to *TV Guide* with every television set, or a film rental membership with each VCR.

Beginners often make the mistake of thinking that a single promotional effort like a Grand Opening celebration is sufficient to maintain sales volume. Or they may fail to give the promotion enough advertising in enough places to really bring in the crowds. It is usually necessary to stage a sequence of promotions, year after year. When you do stage one, however, use as many devices in concert as you can think of: caps and T-shirts, balloon rides, clowns, free food, and a celebrity all together at your anniversary celebration will bring you more business than the same devices spread among several promotions.

Publicity

Advertising is promotion you pay for. **Publicity** is free. You get publicity by thinking of a newsworthy event. Just the opening of your pizza business is not likely to be sufficient. But if you create the "world's biggest pizza" and invite photographers, media people, and the press to see, sniff, and taste, you may find yourself and your business in the news.

Another publicity device is a contest. One pet shop owner put an empty fishbowl in his store window and invited passersby to "Count the Invisible Fish!" A smaller sign invited them to come in and fill in an application blank. The strategy generated a great deal of free word-of-mouth publicity.

Travel agencies often sponsor free travel films. A ski shop might sponsor a ski trip, perhaps with free lessons thrown in. The trick in generating publicity is to think of something that relates to your business without actually trying to sell something.

Check your local library's card catalog under "Publicity" for books with ideas for whole campaigns. If your budget permits, you might hire a publicity agent to develop a single event or a whole campaign. If you cannot afford a campaign on your own, your merchants' association or Chamber of Commerce may cooperate with an event that involves a whole business district or town.

Public Relations

Public relations is more subtle than publicity. Public relations campaigns are designed to make people think well of your business. You may participate in a United Fund campaign, collect blankets and food for the homeless, sponsor a Little League or bowling team, or participate in some community event like a fireworks display or arts festival.

Good public relations is more than a series of strategies; it is an attitude of wanting to put something back into the community in return for what you receive from it. Good public relations is treating all customers courteously. It is keeping your premises tidy and in good repair. It is pulling the weeds around street trees when the city does not get to it.

Larger firms engage public relations agents to continually burnish their image. Smaller businesses create their images by their daily actions.

Merchandising

When you surround your product or service with everything you can think of to make it more appealing, you are doing **merchandising.** An ice-cream parlor is merchandising when it treats birthday children with a soup-bowl-sized sundae topped with flags and sparklers and served by waitresses singing "Happy Birthday." Casinos are merchandising when they surround their slot machines with red velvet, mirrors, flashing lights, and floor shows. Hospitals are merchandising when they deck their pediatric wards with bright posters and have the children's meals served by aides wearing clown suits.

Merchandising includes lighting, color, music, carpets, display materials, and uniforms. Century 21 is merchandising when it dresses its agents in yellow blazers. McDonald's is merchandising when it has its golden arches printed on every bag and carton and gives away glasses with cartoon characters printed on them. A produce store is merchandising when it stacks the oranges in pyramids. Merchandising includes the black velvet cloth a jeweler puts beneath a diamond bracelet he is showing. It is the handsome binder into which the insurance agent puts your policy.

In short, merchandising is everything you can think of to spotlight your product and show it off.

Remember that nothing in business is stationary. You are always selling to a passing parade. Each year brings a crop of newly licensed drivers to your auto business and a group of newly retired workers to your travel agency. You must constantly appeal to the next group of customers because your existing customers move away, or die, or simply outgrow their need for your product. Attrition is a part of the business scene; you can never rest on what you did last year.

Every year brings new competition. To depend on last year's promotion—or even last month's—is to fall behind. The parade will pass you by.

Bringing Your Business to the Customers

So far, we have talked about bringing customers to your business. Sometimes all the strategies you can try are not enough. Insufficient volume underlies most business failures. If business is failing to come to you, you have to go out and get it.

Go Where the Customers Are

First, decide where the business is. Where would you find the customers who are not coming in?

○ For a delicatessen: Who would purchase food if I delivered it?
○ For a beauty shop: Who would use my services if I offered shampoos and manicures at home?
○ For an auto repair: Where would I find customers for on-the-spot oil changes or tune-ups?

Route Delivery

Home delivery of bread, milk, fresh produce, and even medical care seems quaint and old-fashioned today. The cost is high. Still, innovative entrepreneurs can think of new opportunities for home delivery:

bartending, disk jockeying, decorating, rug cleaning. Carbonated beverages, bottled water, and even potato chips are being delivered to homes and businesses every day. Give some thought to whether some part of your business could take this route.

Shows and Demonstrations in the Home

This kind of merchandising has made household names out of companies like Tupperware, Avon, and Mary Kay. Clothing, home decor, leather goods, baskets, crystal, cookware, and any number of products can be sold by home demonstrations. Can yours?

Enlist homeowners by offering them a free item for inviting people over for refreshments and a demonstration. Conduct a drawing—it will give you the names and addresses of attendees. Contact them and suggest that they hold a demonstration, too; keep an endless chain of demonstrations going.

Make your demonstrations clever, interesting, and useful. Give the attendees a good time. If you are a florist, teach some tricks of the flower-arranging trade. If you run a restaurant, teach garnishing tricks. If you sell clothing, teach color coordination or accessorizing. Your home demonstration need not sell products directly; it can be a public service that will incline people to patronize your business.

Be a Speaker

Contact a library, community center, or senior citizens' center about giving a public-service lecture. If you sell insurance, talk about fire prevention or first-aid techniques. If you sell investments, explain the workings of the stock market. A landscaper can talk about garden planning or how to grow flowers in shady places. A heating appliance dealer can give insulation tips. The opportunities to share your knowledge and gain business in doing so are endless. You may even find yourself on TV. Bring a good supply of business cards. Hand out literature, and be sure it has your name and address on it. Get attendees to sign in with their names and addresses for follow-up, perhaps by offering a drawing or a free personal consultation.

Mall Shows

Shopping malls are the village squares of today. They are always looking for ways to entertain their customers: karate demonstrations, aerobic dancing lessons, talent shows, cooking fairs. Include lights, music, bright colors, and glitter. Provide taste, aroma, touch.

Remember to keep the show moving. Many of the audience will be strollers pausing for a short break. Consider hiring a professional demonstrator or a show-business personality. Consider lighting, sound, backdrops, display easels, and timing.

Fashion Shows

You can bring a fashion show to a mall, but consider other likely locations such as colleges, conventions, clubs, restaurants. The focus can be men's, women's, or children's fashions, maternity or seasonal fashions, sports attire. You need not sell clothing yourself—maybe you sell sporting goods or accessories. Try a theme: fashion in your living room (furniture); fashion and food; fashion with flowers. Enlist club members as models—people will turn out to see their friends.

Trade Exhibits

If you sell to industrial or commercial clients, you can find them at trade conventions and exhibits. Write to trade organizations (your library will have a directory) and ask for the dates of regional meetings. Reserve early for the best locations. The rental charge for space is usually proportional to expected traffic—$75 to $750.

Inquire about the purpose of the show. Is it for selling products on the spot? For taking orders? For making contacts? Have people sign in with their names and addresses (a prize drawing helps), and collect their business cards for follow-up by phone or in person.

Find out in advance what materials you'll need. Is a backdrop provided? A sign? You may need to bring your own projectors, extension cords, ashtrays, lights, even carpet. Folding chairs for tired walkers may encourage people to pause at your exhibit. Veteran exhibitors bring a tool kit, tacks, tape, staple gun, extra pens and paper, and coins for the pay phone. Don't forget the product! Bring more literature than you think you'll need. If you expect to attend many trade shows, have a professional designer create a portable exhibit booth for you.

It is difficult to estimate whether trade shows are worthwhile. They may not generate enough direct sales to cover space rentals, travel, meals, and hotel fees. Long-run benefits such as publicizing your name and business may justify your participation nonetheless.

Sidewalk Sales

Downtown merchants and mall tradespeople often combine forces to generate customers for a sale by displaying merchandise outside their stores. Usually the event is publicized with special mailings or newspaper supplements that individual merchants might not be able to afford. These sales give you a chance to sell slower-moving merchandise and out-of-season items. Customers usually expect bargains.

Sidewalk sales can introduce your products to people who might not ordinarily enter your store. The objective is to generate repeat business at a later time through bargain prices, opportunities to browse, and impulse purchases.

Parade Floats

Barnum and Bailey knew the value of a parade! This is not the time to be too commercial; sponsor a float for some community organization: Scouts, the emergency squad, the library, or the animal shelter. Consider parades an opportunity for public relations rather than advertising.

Door-to-Door Canvassing

Vacuum cleaners and Girl Scout cookies are sold door-to-door. This is called cold canvassing: when you knock on a door you have no idea whether the person who answers is a potential purchaser. If you have the courage to knock on strangers' doors and the fortitude to withstand rejection, canvassing can be rewarding. There are good and bad times to canvass door-to-door. Too early in the morning is disturbing. Late in the evening, people may be reluctant to open the door to strangers. The prime time is 10 A.M. to 4 P.M. More families are likely to be at home on Saturdays than during the week—with so many mothers working, a weekday call may find you selling to the baby-sitter.

CHAPTER ELEVEN

Making the Sale

KEY TERMS

closing
preparation

presentation
prospecting

Selling is the personal part of marketing. Advertising, publicity, sales promotions, and merchandising are directed at the general public. Only when the sale is being made do seller and prospect meet face-to-face. In selling, you engage the customer in dialogue—one on one. It's now up to you to persuade the customer to buy. Business veterans call this the moment of truth.

What Is Salesmanship?

Some experts in selling, including Dottie Walters, a veteran in sales training, suggest that "salesmanship" is an out-of-date term. They prefer to call it "selling power" or "selling skill." Certainly sales"man"ship is not a male prerogative. Many top salespeople are women, and the U.S. Census Bureau recently reported that five out of six new U.S. businesses are started by women.

Many titles have been used for the people who sell goods and services: sales representative, sales agent, company representative, account executive, sales consultant, sales associate, even "senior account marketing development representative." For simplicity, this text uses "salesperson" or "sales representative," but when it comes to the skill of selling, no word yet devised says it as well as "salesmanship."

Salesmen have introduced cash registers, refrigerators, automobiles, vacuum cleaners, air conditioners, photocopiers, and computers to the public and to business. Salesmanship offers benefits not found in advertising and promotion. Advertising says, "We have it." Salesmanship makes the customer feel, "I want it." Salesmanship adjusts its message to the individual, emphasizing low price to the bargain hunter, durability and service to the seeker of quality. A printed page can't adjust to the reader's headache; a TV ad can't adjust to the viewer's bad mood. A salesman can.

Do You Need a Sales Force?

To decide whether to hire a sales force or do the selling yourself, reexamine your marketing plan. How many of your strategies involve salesmanship? Can you do all that selling yourself and still have time to manage the business? Then, ask yourself:

○ How important are salespeople to my business?

○ How large a sales force do I need?

○ Should I have inside salespeople? Outside salespeople who call on customers? Salespeople who work only at trade shows or promotional events?

○ Should salesmen telephone "cold" for prospects ("inside telemarketing"), or should they merely respond to incoming calls initiated by prospective customers?

○ Should my route drivers receive sales training?

○ Which of my products or services require salesmanship and which do not?

No promotional medium can beat a skilled salesperson at getting the customer to buy. Salesmanship collects the money and delivers the goods as no promotional effort can.

Keep in mind, though, that products that are simple and well known (peanut butter, for example) require less salesmanship than complex products for which the customer needs explanations or instructions (computers, for example). Impulse items require little salesmanship; if they don't sell themselves, they won't sell. Hanging Scotch tape and batteries on racks by the checkout counter will stimulate a certain number of purchases with no help from any sales personnel.

New products take more selling. Someone is needed to show the browser how simply the VCR can be programmed, how brilliant the stereo sound is, how the dishwasher works. Printed instructions are no substitute for knowledgeable explanation. (On the other hand, they are better than fumbling inexperience.) Salesmanship turns browsers into buyers.

Observation will show you that the average salesperson—whether he or she is selling men's suits, cars, or condominiums—has little professional expertise. As you read this chapter, consider how you could polish up your own selling skills and those of your employees to make your business shine.

Backing Up the Sales Effort

Salesmanship is much more than standing in the middle of a room and offering a product to a customer. To be effective, salesmanship must be part of an overall marketing program that starts with a business name that appeals to customers and signals what you are selling. Carry your theme through with appropriate decor, lighting, and music. Perhaps your employees should have uniforms or a pocket patch with the company logo. Your displays should be engineered for appeal, your promotion precisely targeted. Your product or service should be competitively priced, and your business well located for the customers you expect to serve. When you have done these things, you have set the stage on which your salespeople can perform.

Unsupported salespeople are less effective. The toughest sales mission is the "cold call" in which the salesperson, unannounced and unknown, approaches a stranger's door. Even a circular sent out ahead eases this situation. A qualifying telephone call that sets a specific appointment is better. Support your salesperson with a demonstration kit, a presentation manual, literature, and photographs. If a picture is worth a thousand words, a working sample—for instance, a scale-model vinyl window unit—is worth ten thousand.

Ineffective sales personnel are order takers. Effective salespeople are order getters. Salespeople who merely take the orders they get aren't practicing salesmanship. The true salesperson goes after all the potential sales volume there is.

Going for what is there doesn't mean being pushy. Most people have an ingrained aversion to overbearing tactics—the kind that make people say, "Close the blinds; that looks like a salesman coming up the walk." In public esteem, the clergy ranks highest; salespeople rank low—not far above garbage collectors. This image has been built by the many salespeople who are not true professionals.

Effective salespeople are proud professionals who help customers buy goods and services they need and thereby enrich their lifestyles. Salesmanship is *not* persuading people to buy what they can't afford, don't need, or don't want. Salesmanship is making customers aware of the ways in which the product can benefit them.

However, to say that customers should not be pressured into buying what they don't need is not to say that they should not be persuaded to buy something they need without realizing it. A broad definition of salesmanship would include a nurse persuading a client to follow an exercise regimen, an auto salesman persuading a driver to trade in an unsafe car for a new one, or a service station attendant persuading a customer to have the oil changed. The definition of what the customer needs can be broadened to include any purchase that provides a benefit in efficiency, safety, health, comfort, pride, or general welfare.

Professional salesmanship provides two-way benefits: it benefits both the firm and the customer. A successful sale is a win/win situation; both customer and salesperson perceive the transaction as a benefit. When this occurs, the customer views the salesperson as a counselor. For this to occur, you must have a positive attitude toward the product or service you are selling. You must also have a positive attitude toward the customer.

An optimistic, can-do attitude is as essential to selling as it is to entrepreneurship. It is more important than any single selling skill discussed in this chapter. If you think you can sell, you can. If you think you can't, you won't, no matter how many sales strategies you learn and use. To the successful salesperson, the glass of water is never half empty; it is always half full.

The Selling Process: Four "P's" and a "C"

The sales process consists of a sequence: four "P's" plus a "C": preparation, prospecting, presentation, precluding objections, and closing the sale.

Preparation

Preparation includes product knowledge, company knowledge, and customer knowledge. P. T. Barnum said, "A salesman sells best what he knows best."

Product knowledge is gleaned from the manufacturer's literature, product labels, personal use, and, most important, from watching a top-notch salesperson. Hands-on experience plus reading about the product builds confidence that helps you persuade the customer.

Company knowledge is ingrained in the entrepreneur, but be sure your sales staff know the company, too. How long have you been in business? What other products do you make or sell? Where is the factory? Do you service your goods, ship them promptly, accept returns, guarantee quality? Do you absorb the cost of shipping or is it added to the customer's bill? And how does your performance compare with the competition's?

Customer knowledge means seeing your product from the customer's point of view. Observe your product in action. Ask friends, family, and associates for honest opinions. Solicit feedback from customers who have bought the product.

Customer knowledge also means knowing your customers. Learn when they buy, why they buy, how much they usually order, what problems they have. Be creative about finding ways that your product can solve their problems. Remember, too, that dissatisfied customers are valuable—they can tell you what needs improving.

Sales preparation also means that you know prices—not only yours, but those charged by the competition. Watch the sales force of competing firms. What are their strengths and weaknesses? What do they wear? How old are they? What do they carry on sales calls? How do your competitors interact with customers?

Sales preparation means getting the answers to all the questions customers may ask. It means practicing your presentation in front of a mirror until it comes smoothly and easily to you. It means giving customers what they want within the parameters of your company's policies—and knowing when to amend the policies to give customers what they want.

GOING BY THE BOOK COST STEPHANIE $3,600

"Ask us about using our back room for your business meeting" the counter card said. It seemed like a good idea to Lynne, who liked to meet informally once a month with her editing team. So she called the restaurant, identified her business, and asked to reserve a round table for seven on the first Tuesday of every month.

"We don't take reservations," said Stephanie. "Our policy is first come, first served."

"But your counter card says . . ."

"That's just for large parties on nights when we're closed. The best I can do is try to keep a table clear, but if someone comes before you, I'll have to give them the table."

"I eat at your restaurant four or five times a week myself," said Lynne. "I bring clients to lunch there. Now I'm talking about seven people once a month for a year."

"I'm sorry. That's our policy."

Lynne took her editors elsewhere. Between Lynne's business lunches, her own meals, and her group meeting, Stephanie's mixed message and inflexible policy cost her restaurant $300 in monthly sales, $3,600 a year.

Prospecting

Prospecting consists of continually seeking potential customers to whom you can address your sales message. Prospecting is developing both a customer list and a potential customer list. To be effective, prospecting must be selective. Numbers alone do not count; you need a list of people who are likely to buy. Not everyone is a good prospect. The good prospect has:

○ A need for your product or service

○ The ability to pay for it

○ The authority to buy it

You do not want to waste time on poor prospects, so your first task is to qualify your prospect. Suppose you are representing a printing firm. You would begin your sales call by asking, "Would you please direct me to the person who orders the company stationery? What is that person's name?" Be sure the person you are directed to has purchasing authority—that is, the authority to decide whom the company will order from. If you are selling real estate, before showing a property you should know your prospect's approximate income, the amount of down payment that person has access to, and, if possible, his or her past credit experience.

FINDING SALES LEADS: TIPS FROM A PRO

○ First, sell yourself. (If you don't believe in it, you can't sell it.)

○ Sell your family. (If it's good, they need it too.)

○ Sell your neighbors. Ask each to give you a referral.

○ Sell your friends. Use your address book, and get referrals from your friends.

○ Talk to people everywhere. Hand them your card; ask for theirs. Help them.

○ Join a club and use the membership list. Join several clubs. Be active.

○ Subscribe to magazines in your field. Become an expert. Get leads from advertisers and people mentioned in editorials. Write articles for these magazines. Become famous.

○ Obtain published lists, deed recordings, business license lists.

○ Join a business organization. Exchange business cards everywhere.

○ Ask present customers to refer you to someone else. Don't leave a sale without referrals. Offer a gift.

○ Subscribe to bureau reports, *Dodge Reports*.

○ As an expert in your field, offer your services as a free speaker. Collect business cards from attendees. Hold a drawing and offer a gift.

○ Be of real help to a friend, to a service organization, to a church, to a charity, to everyone you know.

○ Study your checkbook for the names of people who need your service. Use your purchases to make sales.

○ Attend conventions, rallies, get business cards. Call people shortly after the event, before the contact wears off.

Presentation

Presentation is the step in which you bring the customer together with the product. Presentation is step three; only amateurs make it step one. Your sales presentation may be a memorized message, it may follow an outline, or you can make it up as you go along. A memorized message tends to sound "canned," but an impromptu message may omit important points. The best method is to outline your message, then memorize the outline. Your outline may consist of major steps:

1. Qualify
2. Mention benefits of ownership
3. Get agreement
4. Ask for order

Suppose you are selling swimming pools. In step 1 you would ask, "Do you own a home with a backyard at least [whatever dimension is needed for the pool]?" If the prospect is qualified, you would go on to step 2: "Fun and exercise for the whole family"; "No traffic hassles driving to the beach"; "You can feel secure about the safety of the water—did you see

○ Congratulate people on special events. Write to them.

○ Use the Yellow Pages. Use classified ads. Get leads from them.

○ Use directories, yearbooks, lists of members.

○ Think of persons neglected by other salespeople.

○ Sell every salesperson who calls on you. It's easy, interesting, and often amusing.

○ Exchange ideas with everyone; exchange prospects with other, noncompeting salespeople.

○ Keep a pad and pencil or a cassette recorder in your car. Note ideas at red lights. Keep a recorder by your bed to capture those great midnight inspirations.

○ Attend seminars. Buy three tickets and take prospects as guests.

○ Call on your competitors' customers. Never criticize or run down a competitor. Offer something new.

○ Join a church and take part in helping others.

○ Find a youth group you can help.

○ Go through your old prospect files and call on them again. Be interested in them.

○ Publish a newsletter. Mail it to clients and prospects.

○ Advertise. Try to barter your product or service for advertising space.

○ Sell additional items to your current customers.

○ Follow up on customers who have stopped buying from you.

○ Use your mind to continue this list. It is endless.

Adapted from: Dottie Walters, *Never Underestimate the Selling Power of a Woman*, Los Angeles: Wilshire Books. Used by permission.

---

that TV special on beach pollution?" Then (step 3), you seek agreement: "That's what you want for your children, isn't it?" Finally, you ask for the order in a way that assumes the customer will order: "What size pool do you need?"

Another kind of presentation uses a series of questions to lead the customer into the purchase:

SALESPERSON: Which is more important to you: paint that dries quickly or paint that resists cracking or chipping?

PROSPECT: Chip resistance.

SALESPERSON: Would you try the paint that's guaranteed for ten years right here on the label? [Points to label while handing gallon of paint to customer]

PROSPECT: I see — for ten years — hmmmm.

SALESPERSON: Ms. Jones, who owns the candy store, covered her entire wall with just two gallons. What size area do you need to paint?

PROSPECT: My store's a little smaller than hers.

SALESPERSON: Great! Two gallons will be enough to cover your walls and your storage area too! That means you can save money with our second-gallon-at-half-price offer. Now, do you want to spruce up only two rooms, or do you want to quadruple your savings and paint the apartment upstairs too? Then you can relax for the next ten years.

Your presentation must mention benefits in terms that are meaningful to the customers. You don't just say, "This car has two inches of fireproof foam insulation." You say, "We add that insulation so that you'll be warmer in winter, your air conditioner won't have to work so hard in the summer, and you won't have to scream for the kids in the back seat to hear you."

Then you seek agreement. "Won't it be nice to really hear your car stereo?" Or, "That's a nice feature to have, isn't it?" As you ask, you use body language to coax a "yes" from the prospect; you smile, you nod slowly, you glance at the car, then at the prospect. Or you say, "Don't you agree—you want a quiet ride?"

No matter how well you emphasize benefits, customers are likely to have objections. You need to prepare for these and meet or preclude them.

Precluding Objections

It's said that salesmanship begins when the customer says no. When customers do say no, it is likely to be in the form of stalling tactics or objections rather than a simple negative. You need to overcome these tactics to get to that crucial "C"—the closing.

CUSTOMER: Well, I'm not sure I feel right about going ahead.

SALESPERSON: I know how you feel. Others have felt that way too. But they found, after trying the Jiffy Jobber, it was the wisest decision they ever made. [This is called the feel/felt/found response; it works.]

CUSTOMER: Your prices are high.

SALESPERSON: [Face expresses regret] You must have some reasons for feeling that way. Would you mind sharing them with me?

CUSTOMER: Joe's store has a cheaper roof cement.

SALESPERSON: Yes, other stores carry cheaper goods than we do. But not everyone provides the guarantee that we do—plus professional installation if you want it, free delivery, and a toll-free hotline. Don't you agree those extras are worth a few dollars? Besides, Mr. Jones, our premium-grade roof cement contains a tough, weather-resistant, long-lasting, polyester fiber that bridges and seals the leak in your roof flashing.

Just one application prevents dirty water from running down your wallpaper, and saves you from getting out the ladder and climbing onto the roof a second time.

CUSTOMER: I need more time to think about it.

SALESPERSON: Mr. Jones, it's supposed to rain tomorrow. Don't take a chance. Do you want a quart? Or, how about a gallon? That way you'll have this quality product handy if you want to do more roof repairs, and you'll save yourself another trip.

or

I know how busy you are, and I wouldn't want you to make a hasty judgment. But let's spend just a few more minutes to cover what it is you need to think about. Do you need to think about the quality of this car? Or the immediate delivery? Or the low down payment? Let's think about it together.

CUSTOMER: I want to talk it over with my wife . . . my husband . . . my mother . . . my dog.

SALESPERSON: Fine. That's a good idea. Let's get all the information boiled down so that he/she/it will understand all the benefits: the handy applicator, the single-unit construction, the rounded edges that prevent scraping. Don't forget the guarantee. Say, how about surprising him/ her/ it? Bring it home for approval.

CUSTOMER: I'm not interested.

SALESPERSON: Well, on the basis of what you know right now you have every right not to be interested. But have you thought about . . . ?

CUSTOMER: I'm perfectly happy dealing with Joe.

SALESPERSON: Of all the things you like about dealing with Joe, which three do you like the least?

CUSTOMER: Well, he takes a week to deliver. He's not open on weekends. And—let's see—I can't think of any more.

SALESPERSON: We deliver in your neighborhood three times a week, and we're open Saturdays from 9 to 9 and Sundays from noon to 4. Let me have an order, and you'll see how well we handle it.

Closing

A salesman who cannot close is no closer to winning than a runner who stops at third base. The sale must be completed and the order taken. You can close a sale only under three conditions:

First Condition: The customer must have absolute understanding. No customer buys without understanding the product or the service, how to use it, its absolute advantages and benefits, and all other aspects of the sale. In selling, follow the KISS technique: Keep It Simple, Stupid. Clarify and simplify your explanations. Avoid confusing the customer with any unnecessary details.

Second Condition: The customer must have absolute belief. No customer buys without believing. He may understand a lifetime guarantee, but if he doesn't believe it, you've lost the sale. You must in-

---

SEVEN TACTICS FOR CLOSING SALES

○ **Physical Action.**   Hand the customer the pen and the application form. Or do something the customer would have to stop you from doing, like starting to fill out the form yourself. Start to ring up the sale.

○ **Assumptive Technique.**   Don't ask whether the customer wants to buy—assume that she does: "Will that be cash or charge?"

○ **Subordinate Question.**   Ask a minor question instead of the major one: Not "Do you want to purchase this?" but "Will you want this gift-wrapped?"

○ **Impending Event.**   Time is short. This offer ends Saturday. Buy now, before it's over.

○ **Narrative.**   "A client was here two weeks ago and hesitated. He wanted to wait till the price went down. Now the price has gone up. He lost a lot of money by waiting. You don't want to lose money, do you?"

○ **Inducement.**   "All orders placed today receive free delivery"; "I can give you the leather bound binder for the price of plastic if I can have your order for three dozen today." Or the classic, "What would it take to make you sign the order now?"

○ **Ask for the Business.**   "Ms. Jones, I'd like to have your order. I think you'll like dealing here. May I tell our service department you'll be picking up your new car on Tuesday?"

still confidence and faith. Saying "It's the best" is not enough. Substantiate your claims with testimonials, laboratory tests, endorsements, surveys. Offer a trial period. Offer the names of satified customers.

Third Condition: The customer must have a need. It is your job to point out a need, or create a need.

When planning for your business, remember that nothing happens until somebody sells something.

Increasing Your Sales Volume

The whole secret of succeeding in business is to increase sales faster than you increase expenses. There are three ways of increasing sales:

○ Increase the number of customers
○ Increase the amount of dollars each customer spends
○ Increase the frequency of customers

These are the marketing principles of volume, magnitude, and frequency.

Every sale should be an occasion for employing these principles. Salesmanship plays a large part in strengthening your business. Coca-Cola increased its volume by training clerks to say, "Would you like a large Coke?" Standard Oil increased sales by training gas station attendants to say, "Shall I fill it up?" Try to phrase the question so as not to invite a no: "Plain or blueberry cheesecake?" works better than "Would you like dessert?"

All your marketing efforts are directed at increasing magnitude, volume, and frequency. Marketing begins with research to identify targets; sales promotion offers excitement; publicity gets the news out; advertising describes the product. But personal salesmanship gets the orders. Salesmanship is the focal point of business: the point where the contract gets signed. And that is the objective of every entrepreneur.

SAMPLE PLANNING WORKSHEETS

Small businesses fall into three general categories: retailing, service, and manufacturing. Before you plunge into a business venture, complete the worksheet for your type of business. Veteran entrepreneurs who have several successes behind them may be able to proceed intuitively without courting disaster. Beginners can't take that risk. As the Chinese say, "Preparation is everything."

Planning for Your Retail Business

Mapping your plan for profit in a small retail business consists of answering a series of questions. When the answers are as complete and accurate as you can make them, you will have your plan.

Why Am I In Business?

"To make a profit" is not an adequate answer. Neither is "Because entrepreneurship is 'in'." Your reply should name a necessary service to a local community that needs the products you sell. Don't be in business just to be in business. Be in business to fill a customer need, a niche, a demand for a particular kind of goods in a particular kind of way. For instance, your seashell shop will fulfill the need of visitors to take home souvenirs that are native to the locality.

I am in business because:

_____

_____

_____

_____

_____

What Business Am I Really In?

This is not a simple question. It needs a detailed, specific answer. If you are planning a candy store, your answer would not be "selling candy." It might be "providing gifts at special holiday seasons to customers who don't have much time to shop . . . or customers who want to make a good impression . . . or customers who need gift wrapping . . . or customers who need dependable, damage-free delivery." If you are planning a dress shop, you might answer, "To fill desires of my small-town clients who want trendy fashions and clever accessories that the local department store doesn't provide."

I am really in business to:

_____

_____

_____

_____

_____

How Will I Get Customers?

Suppose pedestrian traffic is nonexistent, too few vehicles are passing your store, your telephone is not ringing with orders, and the street department is detouring traffic around your street. How will you get sales volume? "I'll advertise" or "Word of mouth" is not enough. Bad advertising costs. Only good advertising pays. As you describe how you will get customers, keep saying, "If that fails, I'll . . ."

I will get customers by:

_____

_____

_____

_____

_____

_____

Where Will I Locate My Business?

Do you need walk-in business? Is your location teeming with the *right kind* of pedestrians? If you sell records, do teenagers pass by? If you sell baby shoes, are there many mothers pushing strollers? If only one tenth of those passersby who could use your goods buy from you, can you make a profit? Is the vehicular count adequate? Will your sign be visible? Is there enough display space? Do neighboring stores look prosperous? Is the neighborhood gaining in target population, or is it shrinking?

What are the terms of the lease? Is there room for expansion? Is the zoning appropriate? Have I plotted the traffic direction at the hours appropriate to my products? Have I compared several locations? How much business must I do to pay for the goods plus the rent? How probable is it that I will do this volume of business? How soon?

The major advantages of the location I've selected are:

_____

_____

_____

_____

_____

_____

The major disadvantages of the location I've selected are:

_____

_____

_____

_____

_____

_____

Who Are My Competitors and Suppliers?

The number of competing businesses is:

_____

The number of prosperous-looking competitors is:

_____

How many competitors went out of business last year? Why?

_____

_____

_____

_____

_____

_____

_____

_____

_____

_____

I expect to be better than my competitors in the following ways:

_____

_____

_____

_____

_____

_____

_____

My competitors have the following advantages over me:

_____

_____

_____

_____

_____

_____

I will make my prospects aware of how my business is better by:

_____

_____

_____

_____

_____

_____

My biggest/strongest competitor will be:

_____

_____

My competitive edge over that business is:

_____

_____

_____

_____

_____

_____

_____

_____

_____

_____

I will be using the following suppliers:

_____

_____

_____

_____

_____

_____

What Image Do I Want to Present?

Like it or not, every business has a personality, perceived by the public as an image. The way people think of you, your service, and what you stand for, is the public image you create through your name, the appearance of your premises and vehicles, the attitude of your employees, the service you offer, and the prices you charge. Your logo, your graphics, your cleanliness, speed, courtesy, delivery, stock, advertising, and public service combine to form your image. You can control your image. You can become what your image portrays.

The image I wish to present is:

_____

_____

_____

_____

_____

_____

_____

_____

_____

_____

_____

What Is My Target Market?

Trying to provide all things to all people leads to business failure. It can't be done. Your target market should be a definable group with common characteristics. It's not enough to say, "I'll sell chicken and ribs to everyone because everyone likes my favorite food." Can you say, "My business serves apartment dwellers earning over $30,000 where both spouses work, usually arriving home late, with a preference for chicken and ribs because of their ethnic background and established eating habits"? Describe your target market in terms of income, age, sex, marital status, education, preferences, home ownership, lifestyle, habits, and as many other demographic characteristics as you can determine.

My target market is:

_____

_____

_____

_____

_____

_____

_____

_____

_____

What Will My Start-Up Costs Be?

Initial inventory (stock)	$_____
Onetime purchases	_____
Accounting/legal fees	_____
Signs, logo, graphics	_____
Rental security deposit	_____
Utility deposit	_____
Telephone installation	_____
Decoration or remodeling	_____
Initial promotion/advertising	_____
Down payments or lease deposits for fixtures	_____
Operating cash	_____
TOTAL	$_____

I expect to get this money from:

_____

_____

_____

_____

_____

_____

_____

_____

_____

_____

_____

_____

_____

Will My Cash Intake Exceed My Cash Outgo?

My estimated monthly sales volume is

$_____

My estimated monthly expenses are:

Cost of goods at estimated sales	$_____
Rent	_____
Utilities	_____
Wages/salaries/commissions	_____
Employee taxes/insurance	_____
Property/liability insurance	_____
Loan payments/leases	_____
Interest	_____
Supplies	_____
Returns	_____
Advertising	_____
Office supplies and postage	_____
Taxes and licenses	_____
Accounting and legal fees	_____
Wrapping/delivery	_____
Losses (damage/spoilage/pilferage)	_____
Other	_____
Total expenses	$_____
TOTAL	$_____

Can you say, conservatively, that your monthly sales receipts will be significantly larger than the outlays listed above?

_____

_____

_____

_____

_____

What Will My Store Policies Be?

List your store policies regarding store hours, holidays, credit cards, layaway, refunds, returns, adjustments, customer credit, customer service, adjustments, delivery, check cashing, personnel (vacations, paid breaks, wages and raises, fringe benefits, employee discounts, cash register shortages). Will prices be fixed, negotiable, flexible? Will you allow discounts for large quantities, senior citizen discounts, commercial discounts, trade discounts, discounts for frequent buyers? Who authorizes discounts, price adjustments, acceptance of returns in your absence?

My store policies are:

_____

_____

_____

_____

_____

_____

_____

_____

_____

_____

_____

What Are My Store Procedures?

What procedures will be followed at opening and closing? What training will new workers receive? What employment procedures will you follow? What emergency procedures? What procedure will be followed if a shoplifter is noticed? If a customer squeezes the Charmin? What inventory procedures will you use? How will you safeguard cash? Merchandise?

My procedures are:

_____

_____

_____

_____

_____

_____

_____

_____

_____

_____

_____

_____

_____

Get a Second Opinion: Have your plan reviewed by someone with retailing experience, perhaps a merchandise manager from a larger operation, or an experienced ACE/SCORE volunteer (see Chapter 4).

Planning For Your Service Business

Mapping your pathway to profit in a small service consists of answering a series of questions. When you have answered each question as completely and accurately as you can, you will have your plan.

Why Am I In Business?

Having your own business will take a great deal of planning and legwork. You will probably underestimate how much of your time, energy, and money will be required. It may take two years to make your first profit. Ask yourself why you want to start a service business. Is it an extension of work you enjoy doing as a hobby? Do you enjoy being of genuine service to your neighbors and your community? Do you expect to gain financial security and independence? Are you prepared to take risks in order to do so?

I want to start a service business because:

_____

_____

_____

_____

_____

_____

_____

What Business Am I Really In?

This question may seem superfluous, but failing to answer it thoughtfully may mean failing in your business. Take time to describe your business in terms of the customers' satisfaction, not your own. You will find that you are not "running a typing service," you are providing perfect letters and reports to busy customers; you are not "running a floor-waxing business," you are providing sparkling clean floors without fail and without interrupting the business of your clients. Carefully consider what your customers need from the kind of business you expect to be in.

The kind of business I will really be in is:

_____

_____

_____

_____

_____

_____

_____

_____

_____

_____

How Will I Get Customers?

Don't believe for one minute that customers will be lining up to buy your service. Some beginners in business find that even their relatives shun them. What methods will you use to obtain prospects, clients, orders, and contracts? If you plan to rely on word of mouth, exactly how will you get customers to recommend you to others?

I will get customers by:

_____

_____

_____

_____

_____

_____

_____

_____

_____

_____

_____

_____

_____

_____

_____

_____

_____

What Is My Target Market?

For a service business especially, sales potential is determined by the area served. How many potential customers are there in the area where you want to operate? What percentage of them can you conservatively expect to deal with you? State the demographic characteristics of your target market in detail. Multiply your share of customers by the average amount you expect they will spend to determine your estimated total sales volume. Is your estimate realistic?

My target market is:

_____

_____

_____

_____

_____

_____

_____

_____

_____

_____

_____

_____

_____

Number of customers × % × $ = $

Where Will I Locate My Business?

If you will be home-based, what equipment will you place in what rooms? If you need to rent space, what is the rental cost? Have you checked the zoning regulations? How will customers respond to this location? What other locations have you considered? How will customers find you? Is there ample parking? Is there room for expansion?

The advantages of my chosen location are:

_____

_____

_____

_____

_____

_____

The disadvantages of my chosen location are:

_____

_____

_____

_____

_____

_____

_____

Who Are My Competitors and Suppliers?

The number of competing businesses is:

_____

_____

_____

_____

The number of prosperous-looking competitors is:

_____

_____

_____

_____

How many competitors went out of business last year? Why?

_____

_____

_____

_____

_____

_____

_____

_____

_____

I expect to be better than my competitors in the following ways:

_____

_____

_____

_____

_____

_____

My competitors have the following advantages over me:

_____

_____

_____

_____

_____

I will make my prospects aware of my advantages by:

_____

_____

_____

_____

_____

My biggest/strongest competitor will be:

_____

_____

_____

My competitive edge over that business is:

_____

_____

_____

_____

_____

_____

_____

I will be using the following suppliers:

_____

_____

_____

_____

_____

_____

What Image Do I Want For My Business?

Like it or not, every business has a personality, perceived by the public as an image. The way people think of you, your service, what you stand for is the public image you create through your name, the appearance of your premises and vehicles, the attitude of your employees, the service you offer and the prices you charge. Your logo, your graphics, your cleanliness, speed, courtesy, delivery, stock, advertising, and public service combine to form your image. You can control your image. You can become what your image portrays.

The image I wish to present is:

_____

_____

_____

_____

_____

_____

_____

_____

_____

_____

What Will My Business Policies Be?

Will you accept credit cards, take checks, provide service on-site, give refunds, bill customers, require credit checks, offer gift certificates? Will you allow exchanges, charge varying or negotiable prices, run sales, give samples? What will your hours be? Will you offer service on Sundays or holidays? Remember that every service has a cost attached. Consider the cost of good service and each of its components.

The services I will provide are:

_____

_____

_____

_____

_____

_____

_____

These services will cost (itemize):

_____

_____

_____

_____

_____

_____

How Will I Sell My Services?

Selling to my customers will fit into my total marketing plan as follows:

_____

_____

_____

_____

_____

_____

_____

I will use the following plan to train salespeople to prepare, prospect, present, preclude objections, and close sales:

_____

_____

_____

_____

_____

_____

_____

_____

_____

What Equipment Do I Need?

List the equipment you will need and its purchase or lease cost on a separate sheet.

_____

_____

_____

_____

_____

_____

_____

_____

_____

Total cost of equipment $_____
I expect to finance this equipment by:

_____

_____

_____

_____

_____

_____

My estimated annual lease cost or depreciation will be $_____

What Will My Start-Up Costs Be?

Initial inventory (stock) $_____
Onetime purchases   _____
Accounting/legal fees   _____
Signs, logo, graphics   _____
Rental security deposit   _____
Utility deposit   _____
Telephone installation   _____
Decoration or remodeling   _____
Initial promotion/advertising   _____
Down payments or lease
  deposits for vehicles and
  equipment   _____
Operating cash   _____
  TOTAL $_____

I expect to get this money from:

_____

_____

_____

_____

_____

_____

_____

_____

_____

_____

_____

_____

Will My Cash Intake Exceed My Cash Outgo?

My estimated monthly sales
  volume is $_____
My estimated monthly expenses are:
Cost of goods at estimated
  sales $_____
Rent   _____
Utilities   _____
Wages/salaries/commissions   _____
Employee taxes/insurance   _____
Property/liability insurance   _____
Loan payments/leases   _____
Interest   _____
Supplies   _____
Returns   _____
Advertising   _____
Taxes and licenses   _____
Accounting and legal fees   _____
Wrapping/delivery   _____
Losses (damage/spoilage/
  pilferage)   _____
Other   _____
  TOTAL $_____

Can you say, conservatively, that your monthly sales receipts will be significantly larger than the outlays listed above?

_____

_____

_____

_____

_____

_____

What Tasks Will I Delegate?

You will find that you can't do it all. State clearly what activities you expect will be performed by subordinates.

I will delegate the following tasks:

_____

_____

_____

_____

_____

_____

_____

_____

_____

_____

_____

_____

_____

_____

_____

_____

_____

_____

_____

_____

I will do the following to train, control, and direct subordinates, specify standards of performance, and reward superior performance:

_____

_____

_____

_____

_____

_____

_____

_____

_____

_____

_____

_____

_____

_____

_____

_____

_____

Get a Second Opinion:

Ask the seasoned owner of a service business similar to yours, a business consultant, or an ACE/SCORE volunteer to review your plan. Keep an open mind and be receptive to sound suggestions.

Planning For Your Manufacturing Business

Mapping a plan for your small manufacturing business consists of answering a series of questions. When you have answered each question as completely and accurately as you can, you will have your plan.

Why Am I In Business?

"To make a big profit" is not sufficient reason. A valid reason for being in business would involve making a product that you believe would improve its users' lifestyle or improve their efficiency.

I am in business because:

_____

_____

_____

_____

_____

_____

_____

_____

_____

_____

What Business Am I Really In?

Think in the terms this manufacturer of drill bits did: "Nobody wants to buy my drills. What my customers want is clean, accurate holes in wood, metal, and concrete." Assume you are not in the business of making whatever you plan to manufacture but rather in creating what will serve your customers' purposes.

I am really in the business of:

_____

_____

_____

_____

_____

_____

_____

_____

_____

_____

_____

_____

_____

How Will I Get Customers?

Imagine that no one is even aware that your product exists. How will you get sales volume? Saying "I will advertise" is not enough. How? Where? Imagine yourself saying, "If that fails, I'll . . . and if that fails, I'll . . . and if that fails . . ." Ask yourself where the majority of your customers are located, and how you will get your message to them.

I will get customers by:

_____

_____

_____

_____

_____

_____

_____

_____

_____

_____

_____

_____

_____

_____

_____

Where Will I Get My Raw Materials or Components?

List your sources of materials and supplies. Also list backup sources. Be sure you have price lists from all potential suppliers.

I will get my raw materials/components from:

_____

_____

_____

_____

_____

_____

_____

_____

_____

_____

_____

_____

_____

_____

_____

_____

Where Will I Locate My Factory?

If you will be using bulky or heavy materials, locate near the source to minimize shipping costs. Otherwise, locate near your markets. Other considerations in selecting a manufacturing site are transportation requirements (incoming and outgoing), taxes, and availability of labor, power, and land.

When you have selected a site, consider the terms of the lease, zoning requirements, environmental requirements. Have you compared several sites? How much business will you have to do to pay for your materials/components, wages, and rent?

The advantages of my chosen location are:

_____

_____

_____

_____

_____

The disadvantages of my chosen location are:

_____

_____

_____

_____

_____

_____

What Special Equipment Will I Need To Make My Product?

List your major pieces of equipment, the vendors from whom you will obtain them, and the price including shipping, installation, and employee training. Have you considered used equipment? Leased equipment?

What Will My Target Market Be?

A manufacturing business usually draws its customers from a much wider geographic area than is possible for a retail or service business. Even so, your product should be targeted for a definable market group with common characteristics. Describe your consumer target market as discussed in Chapter 9. For industrial products, describe your target market in terms of type of industry, Standard Industrial Code classification, shipping requirements, order size, speed of delivery, payment habits, method of placing orders, and other characteristics.

My target market is:

_____

_____

_____

_____

_____

_____

_____

_____

_____

_____

_____

_____

_____

What Will My Start-Up Costs Be?

Engineering	$_____
Surveying	_____
Architects' fees	_____
Permits	_____
Legal fees/patents	_____
Initial manufacturing supplies	_____
Recruitment expenses	_____
Setup, freight, shipping	_____
Onetime purchases	_____
Accounting	_____
Signs, logo, graphics	_____
Rental security deposit	_____
Utility deposit	_____
Telephone installation	_____
Initial promotion/advertising	_____
Down payments or lease deposits for vehicles and equipment	_____
Operating cash	_____
TOTAL	$_____

I expect to get this money from:

_____

_____

_____

_____

_____

_____

_____

_____

_____

Will My Cash Intake Exceed My Cash Outgo?

My estimated monthly sales
  volume is $_____
Less cost of goods sold:
Raw materials/components $_____
Direct labor   _____
Manufacturing overhead   _____
Factory heat, light, power   _____
Insurance   _____
Equipment
  depreciation/leases   _____
                                          − $_____
Gross margin $_____
My estimated monthly expenses are:
Rent $_____
Utilities   _____
Wages/salaries/commissions   _____
Employee taxes/insurance   _____
Property/liability insurance   _____
Loan payments/leases   _____
Interest   _____
Supplies   _____
Returns   _____
Advertising   _____
Taxes and licenses   _____
Accounting and legal fees   _____
Packaging/shipping   _____
Losses (damage/spoilage/
  pilferage)   _____
Other   _____
      Total operating expenses   − $_____
Net profit before corporate income taxes
                                    $_____
      Less estimated taxes   − $_____
Net profit after taxes $_____

Can you say, conservatively, that your monthly sales receipts will be significantly larger than the outlays listed above?

How Will I Organize My Business?

Draw a diagram of the relationships between your employees, using the charts in Chapter 8 as examples. Create the best relationship you can to foster communication, avoid duplication, and promote efficiency.

What Are My Policies and Control Procedures?

For your manufacturing process, you will need quality control procedures. How will you inspect processes and products? What tolerances will you use?

I will control my manufacturing operation by:

_____

_____

_____

_____

_____

_____

_____

_____

_____

_____

_____

_____

You will need personnel policies regarding wages, salaries, piece rates, commissions, vacations, paid breaks, sick time, fringe benefits, merit pay, bonuses.

My personnel policies are:

_____

_____

_____

_____

_____

_____

_____

_____

_____

_____

_____

_____

_____

_____

_____

_____

_____

You will need policies for conducting your sales operations. Will you allow quantity discounts, freight allowances, trade discounts, credit for returns? On what terms will you offer credit to customers? Who authorizes discounts?

My sales policies are:

_____

_____

_____

_____

_____

_____

_____

_____

_____

_____

_____

_____

_____

_____

_____

_____

How Will I Distribute My Products?

Will you need local warehouse facilities? Distant warehouse facilities? How will you ship your goods? Are they perishable?

My distribution and shipping needs are:

_____

_____

_____

_____

_____

_____

_____

_____

_____

_____

_____

_____

_____

_____

_____

_____

_____

How Will I Train and Discipline Workers?

What training will new workers receive? What emergency procedures and safety procedures are needed and/or required by law? How will workers be disciplined for violations? How will I safeguard work in progress products in transit against damage or theft?

List your procedures:

_____

_____

_____

_____

_____

_____

_____

_____

_____

_____

_____

_____

_____

_____

_____

_____

NOTES:

FOR FURTHER INFORMATION

Chapter 1

American Entrepreneurs Association. Researches issues related to small business, offers educational programs and videotapes, generally supports entrepreneurial enterprises. Publishes *Entrepreneur* magazine. 2392 Morse Avenue, Irvine, CA 92713

Entrepreneur. Magazine devoted entirely to entrepreneurial small business. Covers franchise businesses, legal issues, equipment, profiles of entrepreneurs. 2392 Morse Avenue, P.O. Box 19787, Irvine, CA 92714–6234. Toll-free number: 1-800-421-2300

In Business. Bimonthly magazine covering small business. Tips, resources, profiles, columns, comparison charts for business equipment. P.O. Box 323, Emmaus, PA 18049-0323.

Chapter 2

Bard, Ray, and Henderson, Sheila. *Own Your Own Franchise.* New York: Addison-Wesley, 1987. Covers information needed to decide whether franchising is for you, how to get started, pros and cons.

Foster, Dennis L. *The Rating Guide to Franchises.* New York: Facts on File, 1988. Rates franchises on such criteria as cost, management, requirements.

U.S. Department of Commerce. *Franchise Opportunities Handbook.* Updated annually. Lists franchise businesses alphabetically with description, number of outlets, years in business, equity capital requirements, financial assistance, training, and management assistance offered, and date information was obtained. Available at libraries or from the U.S. Government Printing Office.

Chapter 3

Bangs, David H., Jr., and White, Steve. *The Business Planning Guide.* Dover, NJ: Upstart Publishing Company, 50 Hill Street, Dover, NJ 088201. 609-749-5071

Statistical Abstract of the United States. U.S. Government Printing Office. Revised annually. Contains demographic statistics based on census data. Available at libraries.

IMS/Ayer Directory of Publications. New York: IMS Press. Annual listing of newspapers, magazines, and journals by geographic area, cross-indexed by subject. Use to locate trade newsletters and magazines. Available at libraries.

Chapter 6

McWilliams, Peter. *The Personal Computer Book.* Revised periodically. A lighthearted rundown on PCs and their uses.

Computer magazines: *Personal Computing* seems easier for novices to read than some others, yet contains monthly articles describing small businesses and the ways in which they use computers. *PC* is limited to users of IBM and IBM-compatible computers. This publishing field changes continually—check your library and book or stationery store.

Computer books: Books to supplement and explain the manuals come out every day. Your bookstore will have a wide selection, or check the current Subject Guide to Books in Print.

Chapter 10

DM: News on Direct Marketing. Trade publication for the direct mail marketing industry. Contains news of trends, strategies, postal regulations, and similar information. 19 West 21st Street, New York, NY 10010

R. L. Polk & Company, 777 Third Avenue, New York, NY 10017. A major mailing list supplier. They can help you zero in on customers by age, income, number of children, hobbies, occupation, and other demographic characteristics.

INDEX

ABOUT THE AUTHOR

Richard R. Gallagher is a business consultant who has worked extensively with small businesses. His master's degree is in accounting from Seton Hall University and his doctorate work is in marketing from New York University. He holds a doctorate in business administration from Indiana Northern University. As a professor of small business management, finance, and accounting, he has taught for twenty-two years in universities and colleges. He has published over seventy works, mainly in the business field.